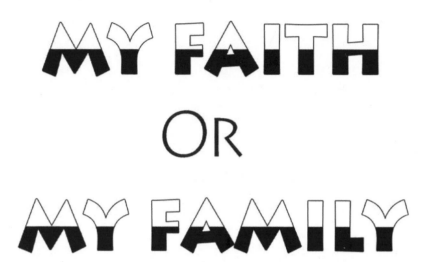

MY FAITH
OR
MY FAMILY

MY FAITH OR MY FAMILY

By
Jean-Paul Tiendrebeogo

WA

Word Association Publishers
Tarentum, Pennsylvania

Unless otherwise indicated, scripture is taken from the Holy Bible, New International Version. Copyright © 1973, 1978, 1984 by International Bible Society.

Printed in the United States of America.
ISBN: 978-1-59571-267-7
Library of Congress Control Number: 2008928431

Word Association Publishers
205 Fifth Avenue
Tarentum, PA 15084
www.wordassociation.com

DEDICATION

I dedicate this book to:

My dad and mom, Robert and Joyce Shobe, who have changed my world and continue to change the worlds of others with their loving, caring, and compassionate hearts.

The millions of people in developing and third world countries who are being persecuted because of their faith in Jesus Christ. Be assured that the Lord your God is with you in the midst of your trials and tribulations. May the Lord strengthen your faith to believe in Him to the point of death.

Table of Contents

Acknowledgments

I give special thanks to my wife Rita for spending more than two years and countless hours typing, editing, and critically reading this book from the time I began. I want to express my deep appreciation for the superb work you have done. Without you, this book would not have been possible.

I wish to express my gratitude to Becky Fullmer, who also spent hours rewriting and editing, as well as bringing critical insights for the success of this book. Becky, thank you for the outstanding job you have done in the book.

A special thanks to my mom and dad, Robert and Joyce Shobe, for providing the pictures used in the book, as well as advice, support and encouragement throughout the process of writing this book.

Thank you to Dr. Ron Sider, who helped provide scholarly, critical ideas on the first manuscript, and advice on how to turn this book into a fine print.

A special word of appreciation to Dr. Tom Costello and his staff at Word Association Publishers. It was publisher Tom Costello's personal interest in the details that I felt called to write about in my life that gave this book a chance. Thank you.

Most of all, I am forever thankful to God for allowing me to see his purpose for my life and using me as an instrument to serve the body of Christ. Teach me your ways O Lord and help me to walk humbly before you so that I may bring glory to you.

Introduction

While we search the refrigerator for a place for the leftover dessert, many search to find a bit of food.

While we choose between the many different beverages on the menu, many long for a drink of clear water.

While we struggle with the latest diet to lose some excess pounds, many lack adequate nutrition to maintain proper weight.

While we complain about the cost of medical care and insurance, many suffer and die because they don't have access to basic health care.

While we try to find something in our crowded closet to match the new sweater, many long for a garment to keep warm.

While we choose which color to paint our two-car garage, many long for a good roof on their one-room hut.

While we decide among the latest technologies when purchasing a car, many wonder how long their only pair of shoes will last.

While we purchase a recreational vehicle to get away from home, many desire a place to call home.

While we build structures to worship God in comfort, many must meet in secret and fear for their lives.

As we wake up each day and go about our daily routines of life, hunger, starvation, hurt and pain are a reality to millions around the world, in ways that we often cannot imagine. In Mark 5, the Bible tells us the story about Jesus healing a man possessed by a demon—a man who was full of pain both inside and out.

After the miraculous healing and the radical transformation, the man begged to go with Jesus. However, "Jesus told the man to go home to his family and tell them how much the Lord has done for him, and how he had mercy on him." Likewise, as someone who has experienced hunger, starvation, hurt, and pain, I have been sent by God to "go and tell" the goodness and faithfulness of what he has done for me so that others may know and believe in him.

Not only do I choose to share the goodness and faithfulness of God, but I also choose to advocate on behalf of my fellow Africans and others around the world who suffer from persecution, rejection, loneliness, starvation, or hunger. Many times it seems as if God is far away from us, as if he had lost control of our situation, or even as if he was dead, but I have come to the knowledge that God is always in control and that all of life's challenges are in alignment with the plans that God has for us as individuals. Wherever you are and whatever you are going through, "Trust in the Lord with all your heart and lean not on your own understanding. In all your ways acknowledge him and he will make your paths straight" (Proverbs 3:5-6). Remember that

God has nothing but wonderful plans for your life. He will always be faithful as long as you remain faithful to him. He said it himself in 2 Samuel 22:26, "To the faithful, I show myself faithful." Looking back over the things that I endured as a child, I have come to believe that not all things are good, but that all things work together for good.

It is my prayer that as you read this book, God in his mercy will open your eyes to see and live the true passion of Christ Jesus. Moreover, my prayer is that we will strive to be Christ-like through the ways we choose to live our lives as Christians in the world—compassionate and loving, with caring hearts for people in need. As Christians, our ultimate calling is to bring peace, hope and love through Jesus Christ to those who are suffering and separated from God.

PART ONE
My Life in Africa

GROWING UP IN AFRICA

There is much suffering in the world—physical, material, mental. The suffering of some can be blamed on the greed of others. The material and physical suffering is suffering from hunger, from homelessness, from all kinds of diseases. But the greatest suffering is being lonely, feeling unloved, having no one. I have come more and more to realize that it is being unwanted that is the worst disease that any human being can ever experience.

—Mother Teresa

Without a doubt, I have experienced some of the greatest forms of suffering in the world. My childhood was marked not only by physical craving for food, but also by a spiritual longing for love and security.

The West African nation of Burkina-Faso, one of the world's poorest countries, is my homeland. My parents lived in Sandèba, a tiny village of about two hundred and sixty-seven people, located in the southern part of the nation. Since a hospital birth was too expensive even to consider, I was born at home using the traditional ways—"traditional" is a word used to describe the way that something is done in the village. The elderly women in the village gathered and used their medicine and techniques to help my mother deliver me. When I was born, one of the village women announced that I was a boy, and everyone erupted in celebration. In Burkina-Faso, having a boy is considered a blessing since he will protect and provide for the family and will also carry on the family name. It is considered a curse to have a girl, even though women do most of the manual labor that supports the farming economy. My parents were not literate and having a calendar was unheard of, so my birth date was never recorded; I only know I was born in 1981. As a result of this, the local authorities chose the date January 1, 1981 as my legal birthday.

Across Africa, babies are given the mark of their tribe or ethnic group shortly after birth. It is a clear and visual way to separate and divide tribes. Burkina-Faso is composed of over sixty ethnic groups, each with its own social and cultural distinction. The Mossi ethnic group, dominant in political, economic, and religious systems, makes up more than fifty percent of the population. As a Mossi, I was given a facial mark that would forever identify my ethnic heritage. Like the mark of identification on my face, my life is full of scars that remind me of my past, no matter how hard I try to forget. As we say in Africa, "wounds can heal, but scars will always remain." My entire body is a living testimony of that African proverb. The more I look at my scars, the more I relive the past in the present. From the top of my head to the tip of my toes, I see scars from everywhere and everything: on my legs, on my face, on my head, on my shoulders, scars everywhere. My whole story is formed by the scars of my life. I couldn't forget the past even if I tried.

Like most Burkinabè, my parents made their living through farming and raising livestock. Since Burkina-

Faso is part of the Sahel region—the transition from the great Sahara desert to the rain forests of the coast—much of the soil is not productive and is subject to extreme drought. Farming is very hard labor because it is all done by hand, and it is one of the reasons many men choose to practice polygamy and have many children. More children means more help in the fields and the ability to farm more land; because of this, children are seen as a status symbol more than they are a blessing. My mother was my father's fourth wife, and I had many brothers and sisters. By Western standards, my family was extremely poor. But, in our small village, my father was very wealthy and well-respected due to the number of wives and children he had.

Unfortunately, I never really knew my father. Although no one knows exactly what caused his death, my father contracted a serious disease and died when I was only two. Our family did not have access to modern technology such as cameras, so I have no knowledge of what my father looked like. My mother later told me that among all the children in our family, I was the only one who looked exactly like my father—tall and skinny with a lighter skin color than the other children in the family. During the times in my life when I desperately needed the protection of a father, I would try to force my young mind to imagine what he looked like. I would always draw a blank and was left with an empty feeling. I longed to have even the slightest memory of my father, but as hard as I tried, I saw nothing but shadows.

It was culturally unacceptable for a woman to be the head of a household in my village, so after my father died our family moved in with my uncle François. As the leader of the house, François promised to use any means that my father left, as well as his own means, to raise us. He had four wives and fourteen children himself, so when my father's family moved in, François saw this as a great opportunity to take advantage of all the extra children—he made us his servants. Instead of taking care of my family, he used my father's money to buy himself a motorbike and to put his own children through school. Most of his children dropped out before reaching high school. Only one made it to high school, but sadly, later became pregnant and dropped out like the others. None of his children were successful regardless of what François tried. I thought this was a punishment from God towards François for discriminating and treating us differently. He used my father's money to make sure that his wives and children had nice clothes and were well fed, and left my father's family with barely anything. François' behavior caused a clear division between his family and my father's family. We were very mad at François and what he was doing to our family, but we were too young to defend ourselves.

While François' children were attending school, my siblings and I were the ones working on the farm and shepherding the animals. This was by no means an easy job. I remember spending hours in the baking sun with temperatures well over a hundred degrees. Although there was wind, it was far from a refreshing breeze. The dry, dusty air would blow in from the desert and would leave us gritty and hot. My job was to lead the animals to any green pasture I could find. During the dry season, this was almost an impossible job, which meant traveling a long distance. I spent hours a day getting to know the land, and I began to appreciate nature and see the beauty that surrounded me. I remember the music of the wild animals—birds, ostriches, giraffes, leopards, elephants, rabbits—and the silence of the wide open spaces. I developed a closer relationship with the animals and nature than I did with people; I enjoyed being in the forest with the animals more than being at home with my family.

Life at home under François' leadership was miserable. Even though my brothers and sisters and I worked very hard to please him, he was never satisfied. He always found something wrong with our work, and used that as an excuse to beat us. François also beat his wives, including my mama. I remember one time when François was beating my father's first wife because she decided to go to the market instead of going to the field. François beat her so badly that she lost her clothes and had to run to the neighbor's house. We could never stand up to him because in Burkina-Faso, women and children are supposed to submit to and obey the man's authority. For that reason, when François spoke, no one dared even to cough. Whenever he would beat the children or the women, no one dared to separate the fight or stand up against him—not even our closest neighbors. We were all scared of him. He was the "lion" in our family and whenever he moved, everyone would shake.

There were many times when some of the women were taken to the hospital for treatment because François had beaten them so badly. François always got away with his actions because there was no good legal system in place to hold him accountable for his abuse of women and children. Even though I was barely out of toddlerhood—I was only four years old—I wanted so badly to defend them, and was angry at my powerlessness against François. I did not really care that much when he was beating me, but I could not stand it when he was beating Mama. Nothing hurts a boy more than seeing a man beating his mom. I ached for the day I would be old and strong enough to defend my father's family. To mask the helplessness I felt, I adopted a "tough" persona, like nothing in the world bothered me and I did not care about anything. I learned to show no emotion in public so that no one would know when I was hurting deeply inside. I also gave off the impression toward others that I was not afraid to fight them. I had to stand up and fight for myself because crying and weeping brought no sympathy. My brothers and I fought against François' children as a way of avenging François, since we were powerless to attack him. Even though we were beating François' children, we were left with a lot of built-up anger since we were not resolving the real problem. Our toughness on the outside masked our hurt and anger on the inside.

My mother eventually remarried to escape the abuse from François. When I was five, our family moved and joined her new husband, Tinkoudgou, who already had two wives. At first, I was glad that mama and I were moving away from François' abuse. Soon after we moved, though, I realized that Tinkoudgou was not all that different than François. Although the abuse was not as frequent as it was in François' home, Tinkoudgou was a slave of alcohol, and he was violent when he got drunk. Tinkoudgou allowed alcohol to confuse his senses to the point that he said and did whatever came to him. The daze of alcohol made him sing, dance, rip off his clothes, and create entertainment for the family. The pull of alcohol was so strong that he began to sell the farm animals so that he could afford to buy it.

It was my job to shepherd the animals that remained. Through rain or shine, wind or oppressive heat, I was the first one up in the morning and the last one to bed at night. I remember one time I had malaria. Because malaria is one of the deadliest diseases in Burkina-Faso, I was very scared of dying. I could hardly move from my bed because of the intense pain that I was in, but my mom was the only one who cared and tried to help me. I wanted to be taken to the dispensary for help, but instead of taking me there for treatment, Tinkoudgou wanted me to watch the animals. He thought I was faking the pain to get out of work, and he didn't really care about how I was feeling. He valued the livestock more than his children—and he certainly did not want to spend his money to treat me when it could be used to buy alcohol instead.

Once again, I was trapped by a man who had no desire to be a father to me. This time, I was mad at Mama for marrying Tinkoudgou. But more than I was angry at her, I was really bothered by the sadness I saw in her. I wanted to see her happy, but her situation prevented any happiness. At times, I would make funny jokes just to put a smile on her face and help lift her spirits. Every time I was able to make Mama smile, I was able to smile. There was no greater joy than to bring a smile to Mama's face in the midst of her living conditions. Even though I was very young, I felt the responsibility to take care of Mama since my father had died. I wished that I was old and rich so that I could take care of her the way she needed. It hurt me deeply that I could not provide for some of Mama's physical needs.

Two years after Mama got remarried, when I was seven, Tinkoudgou got very ill. People knew he was going to die, so they gathered all his children and family members so that they could see him before he passed away. Within three months, he was gone. After his funeral, most of his children left the village for the city to pursue careers other than farming. Mama and his other wives stayed in the village and continued to farm to provide for themselves. However, Tinkoudgou's other wives blamed Mama for his death. They told Mama that her head was full of bad luck, which was the reason for Tinkoudgou's and my father's deaths. That was very hard for Mama to bear, and I became angry at her co-spouses for making things even harder.

Not long after Tinkoudgou's death, Mama became very depressed. At times, she would not eat anything. She was starving herself every day, which was becoming obvious by her skeletal physical appearance. Sometimes, she would talk to herself as if she was a fool, and many times I surprised her by walking in and finding her crying by herself. There was nothing I could do but cry with her. I was devastated by her sadness. Her tears brought all the anger and frustration inside me to the surface—anger at François and Tinkoudgou for the way they treated her, anger that the other wives were making things hard for her, and frustration that I could do nothing to stop it. I felt worthless and ashamed of not being able to provide for Mama.

I searched for ways that I could help her. Taking on

her work in the field was one of the biggest things I could do for her. Mama was a hard worker, and she would work endlessly at times. As a result, she had more crops than the other women did at harvest time, but the strain of the work only made Mama's burden larger. It was fortunate that we had more crops, because one year after Tinkoudgou's death, Mama became very ill. We began to sell the crops, chickens, sheep, and goats to purchase medicine to try to help her, but the medicine did not seem to do anything. Mama spent what she had visiting witch doctors in the village and going to the local dispensary for treatment, but her condition worsened. She was dying very slowly, but I always remained there for her. I was kept busy by running to the well so that we had water for our basic needs. It was the dry season. The nearby rivers were empty and at times the well was either broken or did not work properly. The well was over a mile away from our village. Despite the exhaustion I faced from carrying water back and forth, I wanted to do everything I could to make Mama better. I always told Mama that someday I would make things better for her, that I would be there to take care of her when she got old. I just wanted to see her happy again.

Surprisingly, soon after Tinkoudgou's death, François came and took me to his family to put me in school. Although I was too old to enter school at the time—children start school at age seven in Burkina-Faso—François negotiated with the school officials so I could go. I could not understand why François would make the effort to put me in school, especially since public education is not free and he had to take on the expense of my education. For years he had been discriminating against my siblings and me, leaving us illiterate, and now he wanted to put me in school? Even though it was too late for me to go to school, he was willing to negotiate with the school official for me to go to school? I soon learned, though, that perhaps the reason François wanted me back was so that he could have another servant. Although he put me in the house of one of my father's wives—a very kind woman who became a kind of fill-in mother to me—my status in the family had not changed from the last time I lived with them. Day after day, I ran around completing endless errands for them. I remember making many trips to the well and having to carry buckets of water on my head the entire way. Though at times I was so tired I could barely move, I did not have the guts to say no to any requests or demands that were made. I was given less food than the other children, and there were many nights I would cry myself to sleep because I was so hungry. I ate any wild fruit I could find, and I would drink a lot of water as a way to calm my hunger.

Throughout these hard times, I would sit on my daddy's grave and talk to him as if he was listening to me. I wished so badly that I could be with my daddy and mama. I could not understand why God took my parents from me, and why I never got to meet my daddy. I needed someone to talk to, and I longed for someone to tell me that they loved me, to hug me, embrace me, or cuddle with me. But there was no one to fill that void. Even though I had many people around me, it seemed that nobody truly cared about me. I remember crying so hard to the point where tears were flowing inside and outside of me, causing my throat not to have even enough strength left to talk. I often needed someone to cry with me, but I had no one except the animals, who would at least let me pat them. This is the greatest form of suffering that one can ever face—the suffering of loneliness, feeling unwanted, and being unloved.

Not only was I lacking a parent's love, I no longer had any siblings that I was close to. I had one full biological sister whose name was Tenè. She was my older sister, and she was very protective of me. It was nice having someone to run to when I was in need of help. We cared for each other and tried to help and protect one another. At times, I would help her with her chores and she would do the same for me because we felt very sad for one another by the amount of work François was asking us to do. While Tenè was still a teenager, François and Tinkoudgou decided to arrange a marriage for her. Arranged marriages are something that used to be common in Burkina-Faso, but today parents allow their daughters to make their own choices. Arranged marriages were practiced to tighten family relationships, and were highly driven by economic motives. People would give their daughter to a friend or someone who had money so that they could benefit from the marriage. In the case of Tenè, she was given to an old man who was in his forties, while Tenè was only around fifteen years old. From the start, Tenè hated the decision made by François and Tinkoudgou. She wasn't attracted to the man, and she didn't want to marry an old man, but there was nothing that she could do about it. Despite her high emotions and crying, their decision did not change. Due to the extreme pressure that she faced, she decided to run away and find the love of her life. From that day on, I still have never seen or talked to her again. I only know that she ran to the Ivory Coast, a neighboring country located southwest of Burkina-Faso. I do not know her address or the exact place where she lives, so I do not know how to get in touch with her.

When François took me from Tinkoudgou's family to his family I had no true connection to any other person, and my relationship with François and his family only reinforced the feeling of absolute loneliness. The other children were allowed to play soccer or football, but I spent all my time either at school, in the field, or with the animals. It just did not make sense to me, and life seemed meaningless. I did not care about anything at this point. Although I was not a Christian at the time, I remember praying to God whenever I was by myself. I had many questions I needed answers for, yet there was no one to answer them. I remember asking questions such as "God, where are you? Why have you forsaken me? What have I done wrong?" Yet, day after day, there were no answers to my prayers. I became more reserved in my own world, not wanting to do anything with anyone because I did not trust anyone. I wondered if God was also dead. With all sincerity, I wished I was never born, because life was unbearable. I wondered if God even existed—because if he did, why would he allow my life to be so horrible?

Even though that was a dark time in my life, there was one bright spot—going to school. I was always first in the class and François was grudgingly proud of me for that. I was the teacher's favorite at school, maybe because I was a good student. Despite everything that I had to do outside of school, I always found time to do my schoolwork, even if that meant staying up all night. We did not have access to electricity, so at night time, I would use a candle or a kerosene lamp to study. From first grade until high school, I was always at the top of the class. School was my only hope. I knew that if I studied well, I could become somebody someday and possibly leave the village of Sandèba. Therefore, I wanted to be the best of the best. God had blessed me with knowledge and determination unlike most of my peers. The school headmaster chose me to be a tutor for the other students. I was very happy for the privilege, and very proud of my achievements. My success created jealousy between François' children and me since they never got any rewards from school. But I did not care.

One of the best rewards I ever got was a brand-new pair of Nike shoes. Mama and Daddy were not there to purchase any for me, and of course François would not spend any of his money to buy me a pair of shoes. Most of the time I went barefoot, and my feet would hurt because of all the walking I had to do—it was especially bad when I had to shepherd in the forest and I would end up with needles in my feet. Although he sold his animals to buy his own children Nike shoes each year, François ignored my need. When I learned that I had earned a pair of new shoes from the school, I was very happy. They were far nicer than the ones François purchased for his children, which created more jealousy between us. I was very thankful for the shoes, and I made sure to thank the headmaster very much for them.

Now that I look back on it, it wasn't very humble of me to be so proud of those shoes and to take comfort in the fact that I had better shoes than the other children. However, at that time in my life, I had so little comfort—no parents, no connection to family, no true bond with any other human being. I felt lost. Insignificant. Overwhelmingly alone. Little did I know that I was about to meet someone who would take those feelings and wipe them away with the power of unconditional love.

2

PERSONAL ENCOUNTER WITH JESUS OF NAZARETH

If anyone is in Christ, he is a new creation; the old has gone, the new come.
                                        —II Corinthians 5:17

Although in my heart I knew a greater power had to exist, I did not practice any one religion as a child. The people of Burkina-Faso are fortunate enough to be allowed religious freedom. Most people, including the majority of my own family, practiced traditional indigenous religions, which often mixed elements of Catholicism, Islam, and ancestral worship.

François chose to practice ancestral worship. He would make sacrifices to ancestors as a way of asking for security, protection, or provision for his family members during certain seasons of the year. These sacrifices would usually take place whenever a person in the family was sick, or when there was a crisis in the village. He would also sacrifice as a way of thanksgiving for a good rainy season and many crops. According to the traditions, everyone in the family had to take part in the ceremony of the sacrifice. This meant that everyone had to eat the meat of the animal that was sacrificed, regardless of what religion he/she claimed. This was a rule that François made, and he did not tolerate it when anyone chose not to follow—because if everyone did not participate then the family was not completely protected.

Even though Christianity was a scarcely-practiced religion, two of François' children, Helen and Pauline, and one of my dad's sons, Boukary, claimed to be Christians. Helen and Pauline were Protestant because of their own choice, but Boukary was Protestant because he was mentally challenged. Since Protestants were known for healing the sick—including "mad" or "slow" people—François suggested that he follow that religion. All three were subjected to a lot of teasing and name calling because they chose to be Protestant. Christianity was not well accepted in my village. Many people thought that Protestants were "mad" because they followed a lifestyle free from drinking, smoking, or promiscuity. Some disliked that they held long church services and that they prayed loudly, and many were angered because they did not participate in the traditional sacrificial ceremonies. Despite the hardships, Helen, Pauline, and Boukary not only attended church and sang in the youth choir, they also invited some of us to go with them to the big crusades and to the Friday night movie, *Jesus of Nazareth*.

Most people in my village had never seen a television, so the idea of a Friday night movie really drew our attention—no matter what was playing. Even though we still made fun of Helen, Pauline, and Boukary, we all were excited to see the movie. Hundreds of people, most of whom would never go to church otherwise, came from nearby villages to watch it. Each time it was shown, the pastor of the church, Idrissa

Guigma, would make a call for those who wanted to
accept Jesus Christ as their personal Lord and Savior.
Most of the time, there would be people who would go
down and kneel by Idrissa and have him pray for them.
Even though I still did not want to accept Jesus at the
time, I could not deny the fact that there were things
about the Protestant faith that were drawing me in.
Even though it was only a movie, the miracles that I saw
portrayed—the sick being healed and the possessed
being set free—fascinated me. My curiosity about this
man Jesus grew when I began to see the same miracles
happening at Idrissa's church. Time after time I saw
people get healed from diseases and mad people
become normal again. Many thought that Idrissa was a
witch doctor or a magician. However, the more I saw,
the more I wanted to know. I had so many questions.
How could this invisible man Jesus have the power to
heal? What kind of man could have the ability to free
the possessed? The miracles I was witnessing every day
were unreal.

I began to spend more time with Idrissa, asking him
many questions about Christianity. Even though he was
able to explain a great deal to me, I still did not
understand a lot of the things he was telling me about
Jesus. However, I was able to see the love of Jesus first-
hand through watching Idrissa. Although he was a
naturally blind man who did not have a lot of money, he
was compassionate and helpful to hurting people. He
was someone who truly lived out the Christian faith. He
even started an orphanage ministry—whenever a baby's
mother passed away, people would bring the baby to
Idrissa and his wife. In addition, he built many houses

around his own home where widows and their children could live. The more I saw the love that Idrissa had for the people of my village, the more I knew I wanted that love in my own life. There was a drastic difference between the love Idrissa showed in comparison to the love my family showed.

Out of curiosity, I decided to go to church with Helen and Pauline to check things out. They did not have a church building, so instead they were meeting and performing their service under a humongous Neré tree. This leafy giant tree was perhaps fifty feet tall, and its broad boughs provided a dense shade, very suitable for the church members as they gathered to worship God. Of course, when it rained hard or there were dangerously windy conditions the service had to be cancelled. But the little church prevailed, and although I still did not commit to serving the Lord, I did occasionally go to the church.

Not long after I began attending church with Helen and Pauline, Idrissa planned a large revival meeting. I decided to go to the Friday night service to see the large crowds of people who came to listen to Idrissa preach. The night of the crusade, he was once again talking about the man they called "Jesus of Nazareth." I remember Idrissa reading John 3:16—"For God so loved the world that he gave his one and only Son, that whoever believes in him shall not perish but have eternal life." He was speaking so profoundly about the things that I was personally dealing with, it seemed as if he was talking directly to me. His powerful words pierced my heart. I remember sitting there that night and weeping. Deep down in my heart, I had so many burdens—the pain of losing my parents, the anger I felt towards François and Tinkoudgou, the ache of both my physical and spiritual hunger. My mind, soul, and spirit were stirred. At the end of his preaching, Idrissa asked for those who wanted to give themselves to Jesus as their Lord and Savior.

Idrissa continued to talk, and I started to see people moving toward him. I wanted so badly to go, but I hesitated. I knew that my life and my heart were empty and that only Jesus could fill me. But I was concerned with what people would think or how they would view me, and I was afraid of how François and the rest of my family would react. I didn't think I had the strength to walk toward the altar. To this day, I do not know what exactly happened to me, or how I got the courage, but somewhere in the midst of watching others walk forward, I found myself joining them. Helen, Pauline, and Boukary were there, and I saw them smiling as I went forward. Idrissa had us confess our sins to Jesus, and then he laid his hands on us and prayed for us. At the end of the crusade, he spent extra time talking to us and counseling us about the decision we had just made, and what it meant to be a follower of Jesus Christ. I accepted Jesus Christ into my heart at the age of eleven.

When I got home, I informed François and the rest of the family that I had accepted the man "Jesus of Nazareth" as my Lord and Savior. I could see them whispering to one another, and I did not know what they were saying, but I did not really care. Some of them were not surprised about my decision since I had been attending some of the services. However, they all looked at me and started laughing. They started mocking me and making jokes at me just like I used to do to Helen, Pauline, and Boukary. They thought I was out of my mind for my decision, or that I converted just for the sake of being "religious." Deep down, I knew that I wanted much more than just a religion. In fact, it was not about "religion" at all to me. I wanted a relationship with someone who could heal my broken heart. That night, I opened my heart to Jesus. Even though he already knew my pain, I told him everything I was going through. I asked him to take everything from me and to be my Lord and Savior from that point on. I did not just ask him to be my Savior because someone told me to, but I really believed that he was the only one who could save me. These words were coming straight from my heart, and they were honest and sincere. I had a great sleep that night, and it was perhaps the best sleep I had for a long time. From that moment on, Jesus Christ was my hope, my all in all, and my everything. As the psalmist writes in Psalm 71:5: "You are my hope, O Sovereign Lord."

Soon after accepting Jesus Christ into my life, I began to meet with Idrissa outside of church whenever possible, to talk to him about being a follower of God. Idrissa decided to enroll me in a class where the new Christians met together once a week to counsel and support each other, and to discuss the things they did not understand. We also talked about how to handle the persecutions and family rejection that some of us were receiving for accepting Jesus. This was an opportunity for us to learn about the character and personality of the man Jesus, and to understand what it meant to be a Christian. I met a lot of new people at the church. I decided to get involved with the youth and I even sang in the youth choir. Although it was hard to forget and to let go of all that had happened to me, I tried to start fresh with Jesus. I knew in my heart that he could take all my sorrow and turn it to joy. This was a major turning point in my life. It was a new day and a new season. I had just begun my journey with Jesus Christ, my Lord and Savior.

Idrissa offered to give me a Bible to help me grow spiritually. Reading the Bible helped to answer most of the questions I had, and it helped open my eyes to see and know the personality and character of Jesus Christ. I enjoyed reading the Bible because it was the food of my soul. I carried it with me wherever I went, and whether I was in the forest, at school, or at home, I took every opportunity I had to meditate upon it. As a result, many of the verses became the melodies of my new songs, and the words became my strength and my hope for a better future.

I also continued attending the new believer class at the church and singing in the youth choir. I soon developed close relationships with many people in the church, and no longer felt left behind, lonely, forgotten, or rejected. Now I had a church family to take care of me. Idrissa and his family began to take care of me, providing me with clothes to wear and, at times, food to eat. Though Idrissa lived over a mile from my house, he and his wife came and visited me several times. He had never visited Helen and Pauline at our house, so this extra show of support meant more to me than words could describe. It is hard to express how much the compassion and love that I saw in Idrissa and his family influenced me in my early walk with Christ. I am so thankful to have had such a committed follower as a role model.

A few months after I began the new believer class, Idrissa began teaching us about holy baptism. Prior to his teaching, I did not know what holy baptism was, or the meaning and significance of it. After all, Helen, Pauline and Boukary had never been baptized, even though they had been Christians long before I had. After prayer and deep reflection, I decided to enroll in the baptism class, along with other believers from the church. We met twice a week for three months to learn the meaning and significance of baptism, and to memorize scripture verses dealing with holy baptism. Some examples of Bible verses we memorized included the following:

> Jesus answered, 'I tell you the truth, no one can enter the kingdom of God unless he is born of water and the spirit. Flesh gives birth to flesh, but the spirit gives birth to spirit'.
>
> —John 3:5

> Therefore go and make disciples of all nations, baptizing them in the name of the Father and of the Son and of the Holy Spirit.
>
> —Matthew 28:19

> In Him you were also circumcised, in the putting off of the sinful nature, not with a circumcision done by hands of men but with the circumcision done by Christ, having

been buried with him through your faith in the power of
God, who raised him from the dead.
—Colossians 2:11-12

After a while, these verses and many others were very well rooted in our hearts. Even though I didn't totally understand the true meanings of these verses, I prayed and asked God to have his Holy Spirit help me to understand these verses. I knew that baptism was not about getting in and out of the water, but an inward and outward declaration to follow Jesus Christ. It was a public ceremony of the burial of the "old man" and the birth of the "new man" as we were dropping our "nets" like Jesus' disciples and following him from that point on. Once the class was finished, Idrissa set up a date to baptize us in a nearby river. I do not remember specifically how many people got baptized that day, but I know there were at least sixty people—men, women, and children of all ages—who were lined up and waiting to be baptized. It was an amazing experience for me, a symbol of total dedication to Jesus Christ, a symbol of a new beginning and a new season with my Jesus.

Even though that day was very important in my life, François had told me the day before that he was not going to attend because he had other things to do. I remember crying because neither François nor any of my family members was there for me, while many other participants had their relatives and family members supporting them. Even though it was hard, I was okay because I was surrounded by my new family, the family of God. Once I returned home from the baptismal service, I informed everyone about what happened, but no one seemed to care a bit about it. I decided not to let it bother me, and I kept moving on with my life.

After my baptism, I became more obedient and was willing to do whatever was asked of me. I wanted people to see the difference between my lifestyle before and after meeting Jesus of Nazareth. I did not complain about the chores I had to do, but I would simply do them as assigned. Despite everything that I was doing to help François, he still did not want me to go to church on Sundays because of chores. This was a struggle for me because I wanted to please François and everybody else, but I also had made a commitment to Jesus Christ, to obey his laws first. For me, not going to church on Sunday or doing the same chores I did during the weekdays, was breaking the laws of Jesus Christ.

I tried to compromise with François to do my chores after church, but he wanted me to do them immediately. This meant I would not get to go to church. I did not know what to do. For one, God said that I had to obey and honor my parents. Though François was not my father, he was still my legal guardian and therefore, I had to obey and honor him as the Lord commanded. However, I kept asking myself if it was more important to obey and honor François than it was to obey and honor God. I prayed and asked for guidance, and a passage from Luke popped into my head:

> *He said to another man, follow me. But the man replied, Lord, first let me go and bury my father. Jesus said to him, let the dead bury the dead, but you go and proclaim the kingdom of God. Still another man said, I will follow you, Lord but first let me go back and say good-bye to*

my family. Jesus replied, no one who puts his hand to the plow and looks back is fit for service in the kingdom of God.

—Luke 9:59-62

I decided never to obey and honor anybody if it meant compromising with God. I told François that I was willing to do all he asked of me to do, but I was not willing to give up Sunday services as a way of pleasing him. François saw my decision as a way of rebelling against him and following Idrissa just to despise him. Consequently, there was some tension between Idrissa and François. I told François that Idrissa had nothing to do with me not wanting to do chores on Sunday, that it was because of my own convictions and beliefs. He did not believe me. The tension finally came to a peak in April of that year, when I was still eleven years old.

The months of April, May, and June are considered the hottest months in Burkina-Faso. They are also considered the deadliest months of the year, the months that diseases such as tuberculosis, meningitis, and cholera grip the nation. Because the health system is severely underdeveloped and vaccines and medicines are generally not affordable, people flock to witch doctors during these times for healing and for traditional medicines. Many people make sacrifices to ancestors to ask for protection as friends and family pass away around them.

As the hot season approached, François went away for two days to consult the best witch doctors in the surrounding area. The witch doctors directed him to make a sacrifice to the ancestors to ask for protection.

During this sacrifice, everyone in the family, with no exceptions, was to eat the meat of the sacrificed animal. The witch doctors told François that if even one person in the family did not eat the meat, the whole family would still be in jeopardy.

Once again, I was faced with an obstacle. Eating the meat of the sacrifice went against my faith and beliefs and therefore, I did not want anything to do with it. I remember speaking to everyone, including François, right before he was about to make the sacrifice. I told them that Jesus was able to protect me from any disease—including tuberculosis, meningitis, and cholera—and even from death. Not only was he able, he was more powerful than the witch doctors and ancestors. I told them that I would no longer participate or eat the meat of any sacrificed animal. This angered François and the entire family because not only did they think I was rebelling, but to them, I was making them not be protected as well. Some of the women started to shout at me, cursing at me, and calling me all sort of names. At the end of my speech, I got up and left the family. I went to Idrissa and told him what had happened, and what I had done. I could tell Idrissa was pleased with my decision not to compromise my faith. He told me to be strong and stand firm in my faith. That evening, I spent some time with Idrissa and his family and they prayed for me. I knew that God was going to protect me, and therefore it did not make any sense for my family to waste their animals and time. The word of God clearly states:

Surely he will save me from the fowler's snare and from the deadly pestilence. He will cover you with his feathers, and under his wings I will find refuge; his faithfulness will be your shield and rampart. You will not fear the terror of night, nor the arrow that flies by day nor the pestilence that stalks in the darkness, nor the plague that destroys at midday. A thousand may fall at my side, ten thousand at your right hand, but it will not come near you...no harm will befall you, no disaster will come near your tent. For he will command his angels concerning you to guard you in all your ways; they will lift you up in their hands, so that you will not strike my foot against a stone. You will tread upon the lion and the cobra; you will trample the great lion and serpent. Because he loves me, says the Lord, I will rescue him. I will protect him, for he acknowledged my name. He will call upon me, and I will answer him; I will be with him in trouble, I will deliver him and honor him.

—Psalm 91:3-15

When I got home from visiting Idrissa, François was standing by the gate waiting for me. When I saw him standing there, I stopped because I did not know what he was going to do to me. He asked me where I had gone, and I told him I had gone to see Idrissa. He reminded me that he was the one who put me in school, the one who raised me and took care of me after my parents died—not Idrissa. He told me I had to do want he wanted me to do (which was to participate in the sacrifice and eat the meat) or that I had to leave the house and ask Idrissa if I could live with his family.

Even though a part of me did not want to hesitate to

move out from under François' cruelty, I did not want to make a hasty decision. I did not know how Idrissa was going to respond. I told François that I would have to think about it. I went straight to bed that night, hungry and angry. I prayed to Jesus, as I always did, about my situation. I got up the next day scared of François, because I did not yet know what to tell him, or whether or not he was going to do something to me. I left for school as soon as I got up, and started my chores as soon as I got home from school. I avoided talking to François the whole week, and I continued to pray to Jesus Christ every day to seek advice and wisdom from him. I visited Idrissa on many occasions and he continued to tell me to read Joshua 1:9 which reads, "Be strong and courageous. Do not be terrified; do not be discouraged, for the Lord your God will be with you wherever you go."

Through this time I did not know what to do or say to François, and the tension between François and Idrissa continued to increase. François thought that Idrissa was the one reversing my heart against him, but I tried to remind him that Idrissa had nothing to do with my decision. It became clear to me that sooner or later, I was going to have to pick up my cross as Jesus Christ did if I was going to follow him. I saw my cup of persecution coming way in advance, and I knew I had a choice to make as to whether I would serve Jesus Christ or obey François and the family traditions.

One night after a choir practice on a Saturday I came home to find all of my belongings outside my family's gates. François told me that because I had rejected the family traditions, he wanted me to disappear from his presence. I remember crying so much because I did not know where I was going to go to lay my head. I went back to Idrissa right away and told him what François had done. Idrissa told me to get my belongings and come back to stay with his family, and that was exactly what I was going to do.

Upon my arrival to get my belongings, François was still standing at the family's gate and soon began to curse at me when he saw me. He said that I was rebellious and disrespectful, and that I would never prosper in whatever I did. I didn't know how to respond or what to say to him. I don't know for sure what happened, but as soon as I began to grab my belongings, François grabbed my hands and started to beat me all over. I tried as hard as I could to free myself from him, but I was unsuccessful. I cried for help, but no one dared to come and save me. He then put me on the back of his motorbike and took me to a nearby house and locked me in it. When I got in the room it was all dark. I could not see anything. There were no windows, and it was very hot. It was a dark night for me. I tried so hard to break the door, but I could not. I called for help, hoping someone would come and unlock me. No one came, not even Idrissa. I wondered how many people heard me and simply ignored me. I prayed to God that night as never before, but nothing happened. I thought he was going to come and rescue me as he had rescued Paul and Silas when they were in prison, but this wasn't the case for me. I wondered if I had done something wrong to God, why he was allowing this to happen to me. The only thing I knew to do was cry. I cried so hard that night that my lungs were hurting, and my voice was gone to the point that I could hardly speak. However, despite being locked in that little house with no windows, the words of Joshua 1:9 came to me: "Be strong, be courageous, do not be terrified; do not be discouraged for the Lord your God is with you." After crying for a long time and pouring my heart out to God, I finally fell asleep in the room.

I stayed locked in that house until the next day (Sunday), when François came and unlocked the door. I believe François locked me in that house as a way to scare and test me to see if I would change my behavior towards him, abandon my faith, and obey what he wanted me to do. However, he was wrong. As soon as he opened the door, I ran straight to church for the Sunday service. My clothes were dirty, I needed a shower badly, and I was desperately hungry, but that didn't matter to me. What mattered to me at the moment was my security. After the church service, I met with Idrissa and told him everything that happened. He told his wife to give me some food, but I couldn't eat. I was hungry, but I needed something more than food to satisfy me. My life was in jeopardy, but I was not going to compromise my decision to follow Jesus Christ. In Luke 14:26, Jesus made it clear: "If anyone comes to me and does not hate his father and mother, his wife and children, his brothers and sisters—yes even his own life—he cannot be my disciple." Despite the risk of losing my life, I had decided to follow Jesus and was not going to turn back. After church I stayed with Idrissa's family, while he spent the afternoon praying for and counseling the people who had stayed after the service to talk to him. When he finished, he asked me if it was okay for him to go talk to François about the situation and see if we could resolve the problem. I told him that I was okay with it, so we left together to go meet François.

Upon our arrival, everybody, including François, was at home. Everybody came and greeted Idrissa. One of the women even brought him some water to drink. When the greetings were over, Idrissa brought up to François the reason for his visit. François didn't want to talk to Idrissa about me. He told Idrissa that he didn't have anything against him, and therefore he was free to leave his house. No matter what Idrissa had to say, François refused to listen to him. In the end, nothing was accomplished, and Idrissa left to go back home. After the conversation, I was left in an awkward position. I remember standing in the gap between Idrissa and François and not knowing what to do. I was fearful of what François would do to me if I stayed with him, so I chose to follow Idrissa back to the church, even though he did not tell me I could go with him.

I stayed with Idrissa that Sunday night while he fed me, and the next day I left to go to school, even though I didn't have my school bag. No matter what challenges I was facing, I did not want to miss school. The headmaster asked where my school bag was, and I told him the story during the break time. He was a Christian, so he sympathized with me, and he gave me a notebook and a pen so that I could still take some notes. After school I did not know where I was going to go or where my next meal would come from, but I eventually decided to go back to Idrissa's house. Though Idrissa wanted to take me into his family, he did not know what to do because François was accusing him of taking me away from him.

Idrissa eventually told me that I needed to return home to François. However, for the sake of my own security, I told him that I was not going to go back. I asked Pauline if she could bring me my belongings and she agreed to do so, but François wouldn't allow her to. He told Pauline to tell me to have Idrissa buy new things for me. I told Idrissa and my headmaster what François said, but they didn't do anything about it. I continued to remain at Idrissa's house for the remainder of the school year even though I didn't have my books, school notes, or any of my other belongings. This became especially tough due to the fact that it was the year at school when we had to take the Certificat d' Etude Primaire (CEP) national exam in order to move to a higher grade level. Although I did not have my books and notes to study with, my classmates were very helpful to me. Some of them allowed me to use their books to prepare for the exam, and my headmaster in particular was extremely helpful.

Throughout this time, Idrissa continued to provide the moral and spiritual support that I needed. He was a great mentor to me, and he kept watch over me to protect and fight for me. His wife also helped me by giving me food to eat at times. Even though I was going through a lot of family rejection and persecution, I was okay because I knew Jesus was with me. I continued to study hard and stayed focused on my exams. I was very encouraged by the words of Jesus Christ in John 15:18-19: "If the world hates you keep in mind that it hated me first. If you belonged to the world, it would love you as its own. As it is, you do not belong to the world, but I have chosen you out of the world. That is why the world hates you." Not only was I fortified by the words of Jesus, but as I read the scripture, I noticed that most of Jesus Christ's disciples were rejected by their own families, persecuted because of their faith, and some of them even lost their lives.

I soon began to realize that even though I was going through very hard times, I was still okay compared to Jesus' disciples and some other people that I personally knew. It was just hard for me because I couldn't believe my situation with François. One part of me had a lot of anger towards him, and the other part of me wanted to love him. No matter how hard things got, the words of God continued to resonate in my heart. God was speaking to me deeply about forgiving François and everybody else, but this was a hard thing for me to do on my own. I heard the voice of Jesus speaking as he addressed the crowds in Romans 12:19-21:

> Do not take revenge, my friends, but leave room for God's wrath, for it is written: it is mine to avenge; I will repay, say the Lord. On the contrary: if your enemy is hungry, feed him; if he is thirsty, give him something to drink. In doing this, you will heap burning coals on his head.

Jesus went on to command us to "Bless those who curse us and pray for those who mistreat us," (Luke 6:28). Even though this was very hard to do, I knew it was essential for my own spiritual growth.

As my relationship with Jesus progressed, things

between François and me continued to get worse. I wasn't going to compromise my faith in order to do what François wanted me to do, and I knew that François wasn't going to compromise with me either. As things got worse, I made the decision to stay with Idrissa's family and continue attending school. I was preparing for my exam, as well as helping Idrissa and his family with their chores. François became very angry because I was no longer helping him. He was frustrated with me for my decisions, and he became very jealous. As a result, he came and told me that he didn't want to see me around again, and that he wanted me to disappear from his sight. I told Idrissa what François told me, and he told me not to worry about it. I took Idrissa's advice, and ignored what François said. Things remained that way until one morning François decided that he was going to kill me so that he wouldn't have to see me again. He must have thought that if I wasn't going to help him, then I shouldn't be helping anyone else.

I was sleeping in an open building with no doors or windows, and one of the men (Peter) who was also sleeping there saw François with a machete in his hand coming at me. Peter yelled at me to run. I immediately jumped up and started running, even though I was not fully awake. François tried to chase me, but I was faster than he. Thank God for Peter. I don't know what François was going to do to me, but I knew it wasn't going to be good. I knew I needed to find a place where François couldn't find me, so I ran and hid myself in the hills. I missed school that day for the first time, and later on I went to talk to the headmaster about what had happened. I became so scared of François that I was constantly looking around to make sure that he was not coming after me. My spirit and mind were always awake, on guard for François. I never could totally fall asleep at night because of my fear, and even though I was with Idrissa, he could not keep me protected because he was blind.

François and I became like Saul and David in the Bible. He hated me so badly that he wanted to take my life, and I didn't know what to do about my situation. One part of me wanted to run away and escape from François, but another part of me wanted to stay and finish school. There was also part of me that wanted to hate François for what he was doing to me, but my spirit kept telling me to love him instead. It was only by the help of Jesus Christ that I was able to do this.

One day after school I even went back to François' family to help them with their chores, but François chased me out. He told me that he didn't need my help and that he didn't know me anymore. Even though François' behavior scared me all the time, I still managed to do the best that I could in school to make sure that I was prepared for the national exam, and I did my very best to love him even when I felt that he was undeserving of my love.

The next day, I went to take the national exam with the other students. Before leaving for the exam, I prayed and asked Jesus to help and bless me with knowledge so that I could do my very best. Idrissa also prayed for me, and within myself I was confident about passing the exam. Many of my classmates went to witch doctors for help with the exam. As for me, my hope was in God, for my God promised to make me the head and not the tail;

the top and not the bottom: "The Lord will make you the head, not the tail. If you pay attention to the commands of the Lord your God that I give you this day and carefully follow them, you will always be at the top, never at the bottom" (Deuteronomy 28:13).

The exam lasted three days, and we waited for two weeks to get the results. I got up early on the morning that the results were to be revealed, and I hurried and washed my face before leaving for school. All the students, headmasters, parents, and family members came to hear the results. The headmaster started to read the results by reading the names of those who passed the exam alphabetically. If a student did not hear his/her name, it meant he/she had to retake the same exam next year before being able to move on to the next grade level. When the headmaster reached the last names that started with "T," my heart started to beat faster. I soon heard my name, and I jumped over and over, running around clapping my hands with joy and thanking God.

In the midst of all my rejoicing, I suddenly saw François, Pauline, and Roger (François' son) standing with sad faces. They had not heard their names, and they were crying out loud along with the others who did not pass the exam. Everyone could hear them. I was very sorry that they didn't pass, and all I could do was to mourn with them. Overall, there were about sixty students who took the exam, but only twenty-three passed. It was hard to see so many people crying because they didn't pass, and it was even worse to see the sad faces of the parents, friends, and loved ones.

After all the names were called, I went back to

Idrissa's place and told him that I had passed my exam. He was very happy, and we praised God together. I told Idrissa that Pauline and Roger did not pass, and that they were crying. He advised me to sympathize with them, to do what I thought Jesus Christ would do toward them. God was really working on me to love those who were persecuting me.

The day after the results were given, François once again came to hunt me down in the early hours of the morning. Peter was awake that morning and he was again the one who saw François coming towards me. Peter shouted at me to run, and I ran to the hills to hide for the second time. I did not really understand why François hated me so much. Though François never told me his reasons, I think he was jealous that I was helping Idrissa with his chores, and that I was choosing to obey God over him. He probably saw my disobedience as the ultimate insult. In addition, even though I was poor, orphaned, and unloved, I had done very well in school and had passed the C.E.P. exam, when François' own children had not. Although I knew that was a blessing from God, François did not share that knowledge and chose to blame me for having success, as if I were undeserving of it. For those reasons, he wanted to terminate me from his sight. It was hard for me to see my uncle, my own flesh and blood, hunting me to the point that he was willing to take my life.

Sometime when I was running from François, I injured my leg. I am not exactly sure when it happened, but I know it happened when I was running through the hills to escape. I scraped my leg on a wooden stick. Though it was bleeding that day, I managed to stop the bleeding. I simply ignored it as time went on, since I didn't have access to any medication to prevent it from infection. I soon decided that I was going to do something about it instead of simply ignoring the wound, as it was worsening day by day—but I discovered there was nothing I could do. Idrissa did not have the money to take me to the local dispensary, and of course François would not spend a penny on me, so my leg received no medical attention and just kept getting worse. It was hard for me to walk because my leg was swollen with infection, and at times, it would seep a lot. However, I did not have any medicine or bandages to cover it to help it get better, so I had to just deal with the pain and pray for God to heal it.

After yet another attempt by François to kill me, I sat down with Idrissa to talk about why François was behaving this way towards me. I wrote a letter to François, asking him if I had done anything wrong or disrespectful towards him in any way. Even though I had my own theories about why François hated me, I wanted to hear it directly from him. However, the letter had no impact. François was still the same man, and I continued to pray to Jesus Christ for help. I began to pour out my heart to Jesus by giving him all my worries and problems, and asking him to keep me safe from François. Though I had faith in Jesus Christ and believed in him, my physical situation did not improve. François was still on the hunt for me, and I didn't know where to hide myself. Food and security became the most important issues to me.

Three days after I wrote the letter to François, he once again tried to hunt me down. This time he was not

alone. He came with his two oldest sons and the dog
that we took for hunting when I still lived with them.
All of them had machetes and were running after me.
Praise the Lord that I knew the dog, because otherwise
it would have been a big problem and I would have
been in even greater danger. Despite all the pain in my
leg, I had no choice but to run from François once again.
I was tired of running away, but I had no other choice if
I wanted to stay alive. The only person at Idrissa's place
who was big enough to protect me was Idrissa, but his
blindness prevented him from doing that. Even though
François and his son did not catch me that day, I knew
that my life was seriously in danger. I knew that soon I
was going to need to run farther away than just to the
hills. François' attempts at my life were becoming more
frequent and more serious. I completely lost my inner
tranquility. My mind and soul were troubled and
shaken, and it was impossible to get even a minute of
sleep because I was in constant fear of François catching
me. Even the nights when I seemed to be sleeping, my
mind was always awake.

One morning in June 1993, when I was twelve years
old, François made a final attempt to kill me. This time,
instead of running into the hills, I left my village and
started running towards Ouagadougou, the capital of
Burkina-Faso. I had never been to Ouagadougou before.
I knew a few people who lived there, but I had no idea
where they lived in the city. I knew I had to find a safer
place than Idrissa's house. I was forced to leave the only
home I knew in order to keep myself safe from François.
I had to leave so fast that I did not get a chance to say
goodbye to Idrissa and his family, or pick up the few
belongings that I did own. The only thing I had with me
was my Bible.

3

MY FAITH OR MY FAMILY?

*Who shall separate us from the love of Christ? Shall
trouble or hardship or persecution or famine or nakedness
or danger or sword? As it is written: For your sake we
face death all day long; we are considered as sheep to be
slaughtered.*

—Romans 8:35-36

The distance between the village of Sandèba and
Ouagadougou is twenty-eight miles. I saw people
traveling by cars, motorbikes, and bikes along the way. I
asked them to help me get to Ouagadougou, but no one
was willing to stop. No one found it necessary to help a
twelve-year-old boy walking such a long distance. It
was very hot and I had nothing to eat or drink that day.

During my stay with Idrissa, he had so many people
to care for that the amount of food was always
unpredictable from day to day. Sometimes there was
enough food and sometimes there was not. The babies
and the younger ones always got fed first, which meant
that I was not first priority. There was almost always
something little to eat, but never enough to satisfy my
hunger. There are no words to express the extremity of
my hunger; I was so hungry that I felt ill. Hunger is far

more painful than any disease yet discovered. Its teeth are sharper than those of any creature, and its venom penetrates deeper than that of a viper. At times I could not fall asleep because of my hunger, and there is no medicine one can take to suppress the pain of it. According to Carolina Maria de Jesus, "The daze of hunger is worse than that of alcohol. The daze of alcohol makes us sing, but the daze of hunger makes us shake."[2]

More pressing than my physical state, though, was the mental and emotional exhaustion I felt. I struggled with my faith, because I felt more lost and more abandoned than at any other time in my life—even more so than when my parents died. I couldn't understand why things were so bad in my life, and I needed answers to the many questions that were going through my mind. But I persevered, and I asked Jesus to guide and protect me on my journey to a city I did not know and to provide for me once I arrived.

I walked to the point that I couldn't walk anymore, and finally I reached Ouagadougou right as evening was approaching. The city was beautiful—I thought it was paradise. It was like I was in a whole new world. The people I saw were well dressed. Unlike Sandèba, where all the houses are the same, the homes there were different from each other. Some were two, three, four, or more stories high, which was something I had never seen before. People were driving cars and riding motorbikes and bicycles all over the city. The city was bright even though it was night, and it was alive with activity. In my village, the only night sounds we heard were the sounds of the jungle, and the night was infinite darkness. I immediately understood why many people left our village for the city.

Even though the beauty of the city distracted me for a moment, it did not take long for exhaustion and hunger to consume my thoughts once again. My infected leg was badly swollen, but the pain of it did not even come close to the pain of my hunger. I had no way to locate the few people I knew in the city, so I was not sure how I was going to find food or shelter for the night. After searching around a bit, I saw a lady who was selling rice and beans on the side of the street. I asked her if I could wash her plates in exchange for food. She knew I was hungry, and so she agreed to my deal. This is a common practice throughout Burkina-Faso. Most economic activities happen in the informal sectors where people constantly exchange their services for needs and wants—mostly food. Homelessness is very common in Burkina-Faso. It was pretty obvious that I was homeless, so people were willing to help me at times. It was not uncommon to see a child without an adult, because children are often left to take care of themselves. After I completed the chores, I ate the food and drank a lot of water. My number one challenge—hunger—was momentarily fixed, so I turned my attention to finding shelter. I decided to walk around looking for an abandoned house to stay in for the night. I soon found one with a roof on it, but no door or windows. I thought it would likely be the best accommodations I would find that night, so I swept the place up a little bit and went to sleep. Living by myself in an abandoned house with no doors and windows in a city that I had never been in before was very scary, but I felt more secure there than when I was in the village, not knowing when François would come after me. I prayed that God would protect me and direct my path.

I got up the next morning and washed my face and feet in a nearby river before facing the day. I was once again hungry, and I did not know where my food was going to come from this time. I decided to go back to the lady I had seen the night before and try to make the same deal with her, but this time she did not agree to it. She told me to go somewhere else and that she could not help me. So I walked around and saw a man running a restaurant. He was selling rice, beans, meat, and spaghetti. I made the deal with him that I had made with the lady the night before, and he agreed to it. His name was Saydou. Even though he already had help, he still agreed to let me help him so that I would have some food. I washed his plates and cups and he gave me some food to eat. I was glad not to have to beg for something to eat; I believe it was fair for me to exchange my work for the food.

I continued this arrangement with Saydou for a few days. Once the restaurant closed for the day, Saydou allowed me to remain and sleep there for the night. The restaurant was made of thatch and materials and was located by the street. Because the restaurant had a roof that was also made of weeds, whenever it rained I had to leave the restaurant and stay under a nearby bridge until the rain stopped. The bridge and the restaurant were not that far apart, and it was easy for me to move since I did not have any belongings. Nonetheless, sleeping under the bridge was tough, because sometimes the ground was all wet and I had to stand on my feet until it stopped raining.

Even though I tried to remain upbeat and trust that God would provide for me, life was hard. I had to fight in order to live, and I did not know what to do. All the pain, emptiness and loneliness I had felt over the years seemed insignificant compared to the overwhelming despair I felt now. At least when I was still in the village, I had a place to sleep and a little bit of food to eat. Now, I did not have any of that. I had to work hard each day just to get my food, and I did not have a home. I never regretted my decision to follow Jesus Christ, but in those moments, when my life seemed to have no meaning, I began to question where God was in the midst of all my struggles. I thought my life was going to turn around when I met Jesus, and it did for a while. But at this particular moment, my life was a living hell. What did I have to hope for in the future? I wondered if the poor in other countries were living like me, or if it was just me. I was frustrated with my life, and I prayed time and time again for Jesus to take me home to be with him. My spirit was heavy and felt as black as the color of my skin.

I wondered if Jesus had forsaken me, if maybe I had done something to make him angry, or if he even knew I existed. As I asked myself these questions, I heard a voice in my head say, "Remember Job." I realized that maybe I was being tested and that this could be my chance to show how much I loved God and how far I was willing to go with him. It was because of this voice that I decided that I would get up and start praising God for my situation, instead of complaining. This thought changed my mentality and attitude, and caused me to view my circumstances differently. After all, nothing good can come from focusing on sadness or worries. I remembered the stories not only of Job but also of Joseph and David, and I was encouraged. They all experienced darkness in their lives, but they continued to praise God in the midst of their trials instead of walking with their heads down and complaining all the time. Their stories, as well as many others, brought me great encouragement and lifted my spirit.

My prayers turned into conversation; I spoke to God the way a son would speak to his father. I wanted to praise God, but I also needed his guidance through this time in my life. Night after night, with tears running down my face, my back against the floor, and my eyes toward the roof, I would talk to Jesus Christ for a long time until I fell asleep. My words were the most simple, but also the most honest and sincere prayers coming straight from my heart. It was through those times of desperate prayers that I found the strength to persevere and not give up. After all, I did not have anything to lose. Most people never experience despair to the point where they believe their lives are meaningless. Everything in my life had been stripped away— everything. Dying or living did not make a difference to me, and to lose my life for the sake of Jesus Christ was sometimes all I wished for. As the apostle Paul himself said in Philippians 1:21: "For me, to live is Christ and to die is a gain." At that point in my life, I understood what it meant to give myself to Christ.

As I was trying to figure out what I should do next, I decided that I needed to find the church that Idrissa had started in Ouagadougou. After six days, I left Saydou's restaurant in search of the church. Saydou did not want me to leave—I am sure he was sad to see a cheap labor source go—but I told him it was time for me to leave. I knew the name of the church, but I did not know where it was located in the city. Since I had nowhere to be and nothing to do, I started walking around looking for it. I went from place to place, asking people if they could help me find the church. At the end of the day, not only was I not able to find the church, but I was exhausted—partly from walking around the entire day, but mostly because I had not had anything to eat that day. Because I had not found the church, I was back at square one. I had to go back to Saydou that evening and ask him if I could wash his dishes. I was very embarrassed, but I did not have a choice. I had to do what I had to in order to survive. Graciously, Saydou allowed me to come back.

I got up the next day and started asking people for the church location once again. I continued to do this until I finally ran into someone who attended the church. This man's name was Francis Compaoré. He was originally from the village of Sandèba, but was now living in Ouagadougou. He was a military officer in the national army, and I remembered seeing Idrissa praying for him a couple of times when he came to visit. After I explained my situation, he took me to his home, fed me, and bought me a pair of shoes, a new T-shirt, and pants before taking me to the church. When I first got to his home, I was embarrassed because I was dirty like a pig. I had not bathed in several days and my clothes were tattered and dirty. I think that he thought I smelled really bad—I probably did—and that is why he helped me out with new clothes. Upon my arrival at the church, Francis introduced me to Pastor Jean-Baptist, and the three of us spent some time talking to one another.

Francis explained my situation to Jean-Baptist. They prayed for me, and Pastor Jean-Baptist made the decision to have me stay with his family while they were trying to figure things out. Jean-Baptist had two boys and a daughter. I began to assist them with their daily chores, as well as helping them with the church services. I soon became more active in the church than I had been any other time. I was very happy, and began to praise God even more for my situation and what he was doing in my life. I ended up staying with Jean-Baptist from July until the end of August.

In August of 1994, Francis came and told me that he knew another pastor—who was also the director of Youth For Christ in Burkina-Faso–by the name of Paul Kaborè. I was told at the time that YFC was a school built by American missionaries and the school mission was to spread the gospel of Jesus Christ in the lives of young people across the country. YFC was not only committed to spreading the gospel, but many times they would give free tuition to young people like myself who were either orphans or deserted by their families. Francis wanted to talk to Pastor Paul on my behalf to see if there was anything he could do for me. I suggested that we fast and pray about the situation before Francis left. I believe that good things happen when a believer prays, but even greater things happen when we fast and pray. At the end of our fast, Francis went to tell Pastor Paul about me and what I had gone through as an orphan, about my childhood, and about what I had gone through as a Christian. At the end of that conversation, Francis asked Pastor Paul if it was okay for him to recruit me into the welding program, one of the programs offered by the Youth for Christ center. Most students had the option of starting a welding business upon completion of the program. However, because I had just passed my C.E.P. exam, Pastor Paul offered me the option either to continue with my education or to do the welding program. Francis came and told me the good news, and I was so happy that I could not stop praising God for what he was doing in my life.

With no hesitation, I decided to pursue my education at the Youth for Christ International High School in Ouagadougou. There were about two thousand students enrolled in the school, with sixty to seventy students per classroom and only one teacher. The church in Ouagadougou was too far from the Youth for Christ High School, so Pastor Paul decided to have me live at the Youth for Christ center. I moved from Jean-Baptist's family's home to the Youth for Christ building. Pastor Paul decided to support me going to school with five thousand CFA, which is equivalent to ten U.S. dollars, every month. I used that amount for most of my food, but it was not enough to meet my other physical needs. To earn the additional money I needed, I did all kinds of informal work such as washing and ironing people's clothes, washing cars, repairing bicycles, and much more. Some of my school supplies were provided at the end of the academic year because of my grades and high academic performance, which meant that I did not have to work even harder to afford those things. I was not trying to impress anybody, but I felt very blessed and fortunate to be able to go to school at Youth for Christ and therefore, I wanted to do my very best. At the end of each school year, I took my grade card and showed it to Pastor Paul and Francis. They always told me that they were very happy with my grades.

While attending the Youth for Christ school, I shared a room with a young man by the name of Madi, who was employed by Youth for Christ. He did everything for everybody. There was also a couple whose names were Basil and Brigitte who lived in the YFC center, and on certain occasions Brigitte would give me some food. Madi and I stayed in an old classroom that was no longer being used. I did not have a mattress or anything to sleep on, so I found some cardboard and made a bed from it. The roof had some leaks in it, so whenever it started raining, Madi and I would use buckets to hold the water so that we would be able to sleep. I did not mind living at the YFC center, but it did give me the label of being the "boy of YFC" by my friends at school. I was somewhat bothered by that, but I tried to ignore it and not let that label affect me. I did not really care what they labeled me as because living at the Youth for Christ center and sleeping on cardboard was far better than living under a bridge.

I began attending Pastor Paul's church, and I started singing in the youth choir. I was also involved in the prayer ministry, prison ministry, and the youth outreach ministry. As a result, most people in the church knew me, and many of them helped me with my physical needs. Occasionally, some of them would give me money to get some food, give me a shirt, shoes, or other clothing. I remember one time when one of my sandals was worn out and I was almost walking barefoot. One of the ladies in the women's choir saw the sad state of my sandals and bought me a new pair. On another occasion, I was very sick and had no one to help me, since Pastor Paul and his wife were out of the country at the time. However, God sent a lady from our church to come and take me to the local hospital to treat me for free. As he had provided manna for the Israelites during their journey to the promised land (Exodus 16), he provided "manna" for me as well. Without a doubt, God is the father of the fatherless. For the first time in a long while, things seemed to be stable in my life. I was living in a very safe environment, and I could finally go to bed peacefully.

Even though my life was more secure, I still had trials to face. The infection in my leg raged on, and no one could find a treatment that would work. At times it would seem to get better, but then it would come back with a vengeance. I did all that I could to survive with it, but there were times that it was embarrassing because of the smell and sight of it. The wound was getting so bad that my bone was showing because the infection was eating away at my leg. To make matters worse, I also developed an infection on my head a few months after I started at YFC. The infection came from a contagious fungus that was going around the city. I got it when I was sharing a bed with anther boy at the church. It started out very small, but became infected to the point that my whole head was wrapped up. It would not have been a big problem if treated properly, but it became a big dilemma, like my leg, due to lack of preventive medicine. The lack of preventive medicine is a problem in Africa as a whole. As a result, wounds and diseases that could easily be treated become huge problems and are even deadly at times. Finally, after going to the hospital, the infection on my head did heal, although I was still dealing with the injury to my leg.

Despite the medical issues, my life had improved since I had begun going to Pastor Paul's church and attending the Youth for Christ school. I had survived enough lessons to form my character as a young man. Without a doubt, all the tough moments and trials I had to go through had played a major part in molding me into who I had become. Though I was a young man in terms of age, my eyes were opened wider than those of some adults, and even though I had personal freedom from living on my own, I learned to discipline myself very well. According to Carolina de Jesus, "Hunger is a teacher. He who has gone hungry learns to think of the future and of the children."[3]

Hunger is the greatest teacher I have ever known. Hunger has shaped and molded me, far surpassing what politics, school, and anyone else has ever done. I was so thankful that God gave me the strength to push through those times when my life seemed worthless, and when despair threatened to overtake me. He had turned all that misery to joy, and through the darkness I faced, I learned what it meant to give it all to God and to trust in him with all of my being. He had brought me so far.

I was very thankful to God for being my father. Though I was living by faith day by day, he was protecting me, feeding me here and there. Most importantly, he had provided a place for me to lay my head at night. Moreover, he blessed me with the opportunity of pursuing my education. Nonetheless, despite the fact that life was getting better, I was still searching for something greater than food, or a place to sleep—I was longing for love; I was searching for a place to call home. Little did I know that he was about to begin doing even greater things in my life.

PART TWO
MEETING THE "AMBASSADORS" OF JESUS

4

MEETING THE AMERICAN
MISSIONARIES

*On the street I saw a small girl, abandoned and helpless
in a thin dress, with little hope of a decent meal. I
became angry and said to God, "Why did you permit
this? Why don't you do something about this?" For a
while God said nothing. That night he replied, "I
certainly did something about it, I made you."*

— Gloria Lee, *Hearts are Beating in…Africa*

On Monday, March 17, 1997, the Youth for Christ
center in Ouagadougou became a temporary outreach
center for a group of eight American missionaries. I had
never met Americans before, so I was very excited for
them to come. Two of the American missionaries were
from Waynesfield, Ohio, and the other six were from
different parts of Michigan. Their mission was to
respond to the socio-economic conditions of the
Burkinabè as ambassadors of Jesus Christ; to care for the
poor, the crippled, the abused, the oppressed, the
outcasts, the lost, and the suffering. They wanted to care
for the wounded, the broken-hearted, the downtrodden,
and the discouraged. They came to witness to all the
people in word and in deed. They wanted to live out the
Christian life by responding to Jesus Christ's calling in
their lives. The group was led by Franklin Spotts, who at

the time was the associate area director of Youth for Christ in Michigan. Franklin had been in Burkina-Faso several times on mission trips before. This was an advantage for Franklin since he had become fluent in French, and could converse with the Burkinabè. He also knew the geography of the country and was able to lead his fellow Americans wherever they needed to go.

The missionaries had come to the country with twenty duffel bags filled with medicine and all sorts of medical supplies. Their first obstacle came at the airport. Upon their arrival in Ouagadougou, the health officials at the airport kept the bags of medicine because the missionaries had to go through the security check-point before they could release the medicine. The health officials told the Americans they had to come back in two days to get the bags. Despite the minor setback, the missionary group came to the country enthusiastic about sharing the love of Christ.

Pastor Paul and Pastor Michel Francophone, who was the president of Youth for Christ for Francophone Africa, organized mini-camps around the country to treat the sick people. Churches all around the city, as well as the YFC center, were used as treatment centers. Most of the Americans could not speak French, so other Burkinabè who understood English helped them translate the people's symptoms and descriptions of pain so that they could provide the right treatment. A typical day for the missionaries usually ran from 7:30 a.m. to 12:00 p. m. By noon, the weather was very hot, so they would stop working to go to the "American Club Center" to swim, eat, and get some rest. The Club Center was an American restaurant in Ouagadougou where other Americans in the country—whether tourists or missionaries—could gather. Only rich people and white people were allowed there. The group was staying in one of the homes of Wend and Celestine Ouédraogo, a wealthy couple who owned several beautiful homes around Ouagadougou. Wend had a great job working for the government. Besides that, his uncle was the richest man of Burkina-Faso. Wend and Celestine were Christians who were involved with Youth for Christ and also shared the mission and objective of the Americans. In the evening, the mission group would go back to Wend and Celestine's home and dinner would be already prepared by the cook. After dinner, they usually sang songs, chatted, and shared stories with each other before everyone went to bed.

My roommate, Madi, became the group's chauffeur, transporting the missionaries to the different treatment sites throughout the city and countryside. They used YFC's old white pick-up truck, which was in pretty bad shape. Sometimes it didn't even start and we had to push it to get it started for them to get to where they needed to go. Many times, their agenda was interrupted because they had to wait for the truck to be repaired. There were times that I could see the frustration on their faces because they could not be at their destination on time. Their frustrations taught me a lot about the difference between the meaning of time in Africa versus time in America. I quickly learned that Americans live by a scheduled time and a daily plan. The concept of time was not as important to the Burkinabè. Things in Burkina-Faso operated at a slow pace, and people lived by what came to them instead of having an agenda to execute. Our lives in Burkina-Faso were controlled by the environment, while the Americans sought to control the environment and the context they were in. This difference between the two cultures created more frustrations for the Americans than any of the other challenges they faced. As a result, I am sure the Americans were looking forward to the end of their two-week stay in Burkina-Faso.

Nevertheless, I was very moved by the love and compassion shown by the Americans toward the people of Burkina-Faso. I did not understand why they were willing to travel thousands of miles, leaving their families, friends and jobs, to come to Burkina-Faso and treat the sick and hurting people at no cost. Their generosity went beyond my own understanding and I had serious questions. Why were they willing to treat us at no cost? And why were they willing to step-down as "rich white Americans" to live with us in our dirty and hot environment? Seeing the way they were interacting with people really blew me away, as they spent their time putting smiles on the many faces they came across. I didn't think that white people, especially Americans, would want to dwell and hang around people like us, but I guess I was wrong.

The Burkinabè children loved to see the "white" people. There was a huge crowd of children and adults around them wherever they went. Some wanted to be picked up, others wanted to hold their hands, and others wanted to go everywhere with them. It was unreal to see the children fighting against each other in order to touch the Americans. The Americans, on the other hand, took tons of pictures of these children.

Children love to have their pictures taken. In my mind, the Americans' presence and their compassion toward the Burkinabè was a model of what I call "the Jesus ministry": a true compassion that enabled those Americans to step down from their big heated/air conditioned homes, SUVs, and unlimited food supply, into the lives of people in need of the basic necessities like water, clothes, shelter and food.

I was embarrassed by the fact that the Burkinabè people were begging too much. Each day, as soon as the Americans woke up, there were always people waiting to beg for money and many other needs. I began to have tears and anger toward my government as I saw the socio-economic and social conditions of people. I had experienced the same situation in my own life, but it wasn't until this point that I realized how prevalent the problem was. Even though it frustrated me to see them begging, and even though it was sometimes hard for the Americans to deal with the huge crowds of people, I knew that the Burkinabè people did not have any other choice. They lost their human value and dignity in the struggle to survive their hunger, fill their empty stomachs, and end their miseries. The Burkinabè saw the Americans as "little gods"—as the ones who had the cure for all diseases, the ones who knew and had the answers to everything. During their two-week journey in the country, they treated more than five thousand people who had all kinds of medical problems and diseases.

During those two weeks, I became friends with the American missionaries. On my days off from school, I would go with them to the home they were staying in, or help them in any way I could as they were traveling across the country to treat the sick. Food was plentiful for me since I was eating with them during their time in the country. In the short time they were in Burkina-Faso, I was able to build a special bond with the Americans. On many occasions, I had the opportunity to share with them my childhood life; my life before and after meeting Jesus of Nazareth, the persecution and rejection I received from my family, and of course how I ended up at Youth for Christ. Most of the Americans were very moved by my testimony, and that alone helped build a strong relationship between us. Although they were loving and caring toward all the people they met, I had found a special grace, favor and trust from them. One of the women, Joyce Huffer, even taught me the songs "God Bless America" and "America the Beautiful."

As they were getting closer to the end of their journey in the country, the missionaries began to receive all kinds of gifts from the Burkinabè. Even though Burkina-Faso is one of the poorest countries in the world, the people love to give gifts. Some people brought them African art work, others gave them traditional African clothes, and others gave them African jewelry. I wanted to give them something like everybody else, but I did not have the money to buy them anything. So, one day after school, instead of going to hang around the American missionaries, I went and did the laundry of one of my teachers. He was single and he usually paid people to wash his clothes for him, which is a common practice of those who have money. They would rather pay someone to do their work so they could enjoy their leisure time instead. After I had finished washing his clothes, he gave me two hundred and fifty CFA, which is equivalent to fifty U.S. cents. I took the money and bought some salted peanuts from a woman who was selling them by the street. I went to the Americans and gave them the peanuts. I was somewhat embarrassed by my small present since others were giving them big presents. However, I told myself that it was the thought that mattered most. Though it was not a big present as I had wished to get them, I was pleased that I at least was able to get them something. The story in the Bible about the widow's gift to Jesus came to my mind. Luke 21:1-3 states:

> As he looked up, Jesus saw the rich putting their gifts into the temple treasury. He also saw a poor widow put in two very small copper coins. I tell you the truth, he said, this poor widow has put in more than all the others. All these people gave their gifts out of their wealth, but she out of poverty gave all she had to live on.

This verse gave me some joy, and I was no longer embarrassed with my gift to the American missionaries. I was fine with it, for I knew how hard I had worked for it.

As they were packing their luggage and getting ready to leave for the airport, I remember crying very hard. It was very hard for me to say goodbye to them, and I did not want them to leave. I wanted them to take me with them to America. People had always viewed it as the land where milk and honey flowed everywhere, and everybody was rich and lived in beautiful homes and drove nice cars. America was like the promised land, not only to Burkinabè, but also to millions, of people around the world. As for me, all I knew was that America was a much better place to live than Burkina-Faso. I thought that the United States was a place where there was no hunger and starvation; a place where there was no pain and suffering; a place of hope, joy and peace. In the little amount of time that I got to spend with the Americans, I got to experience something I have never had before. Without knowing the Americans well, and without them knowing me well, we became friends. Although I didn't know the Americans that well, I was willing to go with them rather than stay in my homeland. Though Burkina-Faso was my own country, I was looking for a place to call home. Living at YFC, I was always at risk of having the people in charge tell me I could no longer stay there. I could not answer the question where my home was if some of my friends at school asked me. For that reason, I longed to have a place to call "home" and I thought that America could be that place for me. I prayed that God in his mercy would put me in the hearts and minds of those Americans so they would want to take me home with them. I remember holding their hands and pleading with them to stay. They kept telling me that they had to go, but that they would come back. Some of them left me with American money to buy food, and some even gave me some clothes and all kinds of other goodies. Before they left, we exchanged addresses so we could correspond with one another.

I tried to remain in contact with all the American missionaries that I had met. Many times I would work hard in order to purchase stamps to send letters instead of buying food with it. I was disappointed when some

of them never wrote me back. For whatever reason—
whether the letters were lost in the mail or whether they
were just too busy to reply—my heart was heavy
because I had felt so connected to them, yet it seemed
that they had forgotten me. I kept wondering whether
they got my letters, or if they simply chose not to reply. I
kept writing letters to them until I got tired of it, and
decided to quit writing to most of them. However,
among the eleven missionaries I had met, one woman
totally stood out from the rest of the group. My
relationship with Joyce Huffer was a divine one, and I
had an inner assurance that nothing could break our
friendship. She was the one who returned all my letters,
and we remained in frequent contact through
corresponding mail. I knew in my heart that God had
brought her to Burkina-Faso not only to treat the sick
and hurting people, but to rescue me.

Though I was thankful to have this friend, I was
curious about why she remained in contact with me
when the rest of the group did not. I continued to be
amazed by her character towards me. Deep down I
knew she was very interested in my life and everything
I was going through, and most of the time that was
what I needed—to feel that someone was actually
interested in me even though we were living thousands
of miles from each other. She was someone I could talk
to, someone who wanted to listen to the emotions,
feelings and frustrations I was dealing with. Maybe
some of the Americans thought I had befriended them
only because I needed money and food. Although that
was certainly a fact of my life at the time, I was equally
in need of emotional nourishment. That is what Joyce

provided for me.

As we continued to write, I began to tell Joyce more detail about myself than I had ever told any person before. In my letters, I told her about François and how terribly he treated me, my mother, and the rest of his family. I told her about François' discrimination towards me and my siblings, and how I ended up going to school. I honestly described my entire life to her as if I had known her for years, and I began to wonder if I had told her too much about myself. Although I knew in my heart I could trust her and that there was something different about her character, I was a little afraid because I had never opened up like this to anyone. I did not want to reveal too much of myself to her. In the same way, Joyce, in response to my letters, began to tell me more about herself. She told me that she lived on a farm and that her family had always been farmers. She shared with me about her family—her children, and grandchildren. She told me that her husband had passed away in 1996, the year prior to her trip to Burkina-Faso. She even sent me pictures of her family and the farm.

I stared for hours at the pictures she sent, and showed them to my friends at school. I dreamt about going to America. In my mind, I pictured it as a place of beauty and prosperity, so different from Burkina-Faso. Every time I saw an airplane in the sky, I wouldn't stop looking at it until it disappeared. I wondered when I would be able to get into an airplane and go someplace better than I was at the moment. I wondered what the inside of the plane looked like, and what it felt like to ride in one. I knew I didn't have the money to get into an airplane, and that only rich folks could afford it. But in my heart I knew that I was serving a bigger God who held gold and silver in his hands, who was more than able to take me to America and beyond America—even though I didn't have a penny. So, my prayer to the Lord was to have him fulfill the desires of my heart and make my dreams come true someday in his own timing.

Several weeks after the American missionaries left Burkina-Faso, the money they gave me was all gone. I had used all of it for food, and once again I was left with nothing. Pastor Paul continued to give me ten dollars every month, but that amount would usually last me about ten days or so. I didn't know what to do or where to go. Many times I would go to Pastor Paul or Francis, pretending I was visiting them, while knowing in my heart that all I needed was food. Also, because I knew many people from Pastor Paul's church, I would usually go to their homes too, pretending to be visiting them. Instead of being honest and telling them I needed some food to eat, I always pretended to be visiting them. I am sure they knew I wasn't just visiting, but instead asking for food, and they would usually give me something to eat. I was very ashamed of that, but I didn't have a choice. I was very hungry and wanted something to fill my stomach.

Even though I needed food, I wanted to keep writing to Joyce. I continued to do dirty work in order to purchase some stamps. Letter after letter, I wrote to her explaining my conditions. I was tired of writing to her about my situation, and I was sure that she had heard enough about the way I was living, and what things were like in Burkina-Faso. However, I did not have anything else to write about other than simply to explain how things were for me. I was unhappy with my life, not really because I wanted to go to America, but simply because I lacked my basic needs—the most important being food.

As time went on, my friendship with Joyce grew even stronger. She began sending me some money so that I could support myself. She would send me twenty or forty dollars or more to help me. Every time I got a letter from her, I was very happy and I couldn't wait to open it and read it, and I usually read her letters over and over and carried them everywhere with me. I always spent the money she sent me on food. One time when I had received money from the Americans, I had not been able to exchange it at the bank because I did not have a national identification card. I had asked a friend to exchange it for me, and later found out that he had lied to me about the exchange rate and had kept part of the money for himself. When Joyce started sending me money this time, I went right to the police station to get an identification card. Once I had my card, I walked all the way from YFC to the bank to exchange the money myself. The first time I went to the bank, I was very lost and didn't know what to do since the bank was located in downtown Ouagadougou. I didn't usually go downtown because I had no reason to go there. However, while inside the bank, I saw many people holding bags of money, and I could not stop from staring at them. I could not believe how much money people were holding in their hands, considering the fact that Burkina-Faso was a very poor country.

I used most of the money to buy food, but also to purchase some stamps so that I could write Joyce and let her know that I had received her letter and the money, and also to let her know how I had spent the money. One of the problems I had was the fact that I didn't have my own personal address, so Joyce was using another address to correspond with me. There were certain people who picked up the mail from the post office. However, instead of handing the letters to the appropriate person, they would usually open the envelopes in case there was money inside and then manipulate the letter inside a bit to make sure no one could tell it had been opened already. I also heard that certain places had machines to detect whether there was money in an envelope. If there was some money, the post office employees would keep it. If there was not any money, they would forward it to the addressed person. Consequently, at times Joyce would send me some letters with money, but the money would not reach me.

Although I was bitterly disappointed that people I knew and considered my friends were stealing from me, part of me understood that poverty made these people lose their character and their dignity. People in Burkina-Faso were determined to do anything to survive, even if that meant compromising their integrity and stealing from those who truly needed the money. Even though Burkina-Faso literally means "land of the upright people," or "country of the incorruptible," this isn't the case throughout the country.

Stealing and corruption have become somewhat the norm. Instead of helping each other out, the poor would rob and steal from each other. Surprisingly, whenever the poor see another poor person's life conditions improving, they would rather pull that person back to square one due to their jealousy instead of being happy for the person. Worse yet, the rich people who are expected to help the poor are the ones stealing the small amount of pennies that the poor have. This is a major problem not just in Burkina-Faso but in other Third World countries—people are constantly robbing from each other as a way to survive. Sadly, extreme poverty can cause people to lose their conscience, their character, and their moral values in the struggle to overcome their poverty. I always said to myself and Joyce that these people were not cheating me, but they were cheating God since he is the father of the fatherless. I knew that he was my defender and he would judge and reward everyone according to his or her deeds.

Due to all the stealing that was going on, I didn't know what to do with my address situation. I learned that I couldn't trust other people with my mail. Unfortunately, I didn't have a choice because the only way I could correspond with Joyce was to have her send the letters to someone else's mailing address. I decided that I could pray that God would protect my mail and its contents, and that was the only way I could really make sure that it wouldn't be touched by anyone else.

Through our continuous letter writing, Joyce and I got to know each other better. I knew that she was making a lasting impression on my heart, but I did not realize how much I was also making a deep impression on her heart until her compassion went beyond all my understanding.

5

DEVELOPING A "DIVINE" FRIENDSHIP

And we know that all things work together for good to them that love God, to them who are called according to his purpose.

—Romans 8:28

Youth for Christ does many things to try to help people and to bring the love of Christ to those in need. In the summer of 1997, Youth for Christ decided to send some youth to the United States for three months. These youth were going to sing and dance to African songs around the United States, mostly in Michigan and Ohio. They selected a total of eight youth and two adults to accompany them. I prayed so hard to be among those to travel to the United States, but unfortunately I was not selected to be part of the team. I even wrote to Franklin and Joyce asking them to help me get to be on the team, but my efforts were in vain. I guess it was not time for me to discover America yet for I strongly believe that, "If God is for me, who can be against me?" (Romans 8:31), and that if God had said yes, no one could say no. Instead of selecting the orphans and the poor as the team members for the trip, the children of the rich people were the ones going. I couldn't understand why they were the ones getting the opportunity to go when they were not the best singers and dancers, but I quickly learned that the ones with money were the ones holding the power to decide who could go and who couldn't go. Nonetheless, I knew deep down in my heart that it wasn't God's time for me to be traveling with them. As they were leaving Burkina-Faso for the United States, I wrote not only a letter to Joyce, but also to all the American missionaries I had met before, and I sent them with the team.

When they returned, everyone could tell that they had been to the United States. They had all gained weight, and they all looked healthier than they did when they left Burkina-Faso. They came back with a lot of new clothes, shoes, and many other wonderful things. Some of them could not stop talking about how wonderful their trip was, and how beautiful America was, and all the great stuff they saw during their time in the country. I also soon found out that they had stayed in Joyce and Beverly's house for awhile. One of the adults who accompanied the youth to the United States handed me an envelope and a stereo from Joyce. In the envelope there was a fifty dollar bill, as well as a letter. I also received a hundred and fifty dollars from another member of the American missionary team that came to Burkina-Faso. They told me that the money was sent to pay for my school fees. However, since Pastor Paul was the one paying for my school fees, I asked them to pay for my school supplies and give me the rest of the money so I could buy some food. They refused to give me the money. In the end, I do not know what happened with the money that was sent to me. To this day I have never received a penny of it, and I know that the money did not go toward my tuition since it was already being paid by Pastor Paul. As for the money Joyce sent me, I used it for my food and bought some of my school supplies with it. As always, I wrote Joyce and told her that I had received the money and what I had done with it.

I remained in contact with Joyce; I was constantly sending her letters informing her of what was going on with me. I also kept her up-to-date about what was going on in Burkina-Faso and what was happening with the other people whom she had met when she was there. In the fall of 1997, our friendship grew even deeper and stronger. Joyce began calling and talking to me on the phone. Since I didn't have a phone, Joyce usually called me at a mutual friend's house that had a phone. Even though we still wrote letters, this was a great opportunity for Joyce and me to communicate even better. When we set up times for her to call me, Joyce decided that she was going to call me every two weeks. From the time we talked to the next time, I couldn't wait to talk to her again. Although I didn't have a calendar, I kept track of the day and time Joyce was supposed to call me, and I was always excited to talk with her. I would go to the lady's house one or two hours before Joyce was to call, waiting anxiously to talk to her. We usually talked about everything. I would tell her how I was doing at school, how things were going in general, and Joyce would also share with me how she was doing. One of the challenges I had was how to have any privacy in my conversations with Joyce. There were too many people sitting in the room when I talked on the phone. I thought of asking them to give me some privacy, but I didn't want to be rude or offend anyone.

Toward the end of the summer, I wrote a letter to Joyce and asked her for a mattress since I didn't have anything to sleep on. Joyce decided to send me fifty dollars to purchase the mattress, which was far beyond the price of a normal mattress. However, since I didn't have my own personal address, Joyce decided to send the money to another address where I could pick it up. Sadly, I never received the mattress or the money. I told Joyce over and over that I had never received the mattress or the money that she sent. As time went on, Joyce and I decided to move on and forget about the mattress, instead of confronting the person to whom Joyce had sent the money.

It was very hard for me to keep my mouth shut and not say anything about it. It is not that big of a deal if it happens once or twice, but it kept happening over and over to me. I could not understand why they would take the money and not give it to me. I was mad at the people for cheating me, since I was essentially a homeless orphan. The more I wanted to confront the people who stole from me, the more the Holy Spirit told me to be quiet. I gave everything to God, for he himself said in Romans 12:19-21: "Do not take revenge, my friends but leave room for God's wrath, for it is written: it is mine to avenge. I will repay says the Lord…do not be overcome by evil, but overcome evil with good." So, I just moved on and let God deal with them.

On August 7, 1997, Joyce got remarried to Robert Shobe. I didn't even know she had a boyfriend or was engaged. She had never mentioned that to me either on the phone or through the mail. She sent me a letter along with some photos of Robert and their wedding. She also introduced him to me, and told me a little more about him and what he did. She also told me that her name would be changing from Joyce Huffer to Joyce Shobe. I replied to her letter and told her that I was happy for her. I sent them my blessings, as they were starting a new life together and said that I couldn't wait to meet him sometime.

I shared the good news with some of my friends, and showed them pictures of the wedding. Even though Joyce was remarried, she and Robert both continued to correspond with me. They would talk to me on the phone, and also through letters. In January of 1998, Joyce and Robert informed me in a letter that they were both planning to come to Burkina-Faso with the Youth for Christ medical mission trip team. As soon as I learned that, I could not wait to see Joyce again and meet her husband Robert as well. I was so anxious that not only did it consume my thoughts during the day, but I began to dream about it at night as well. I even started counting down the days until I saw them again. Joyce was a blessing sent from God, and my contact with her gave me new hope to press on through all the very hard trials. As I anticipated the Americans' coming, I began to fast and pray for their trip. I prayed that God would bring them safely to Burkina-Faso. I also began to pray for the Lord to fulfill the desires of my heart. I wanted to go with them back to the United States so badly, and I even began to pray that I would get that opportunity.

On March 19, 1998, Joyce and Robert Shobe, along with nine other American missionaries, landed in

Burkina-Faso. This time three out of the eleven people were from Waynesfield, Ohio (Beverly Gallant and Robert and Joyce Shobe); one from Lynchburg, Virginia; another from Aurora, Colorado; another person from Sarasota, Florida. The other five people were from various parts of Michigan. As they had in 1997, they came in 1998 with bags loaded with all kinds of medicine; once again, the group was headed by Franklin Spotts. They arrived in the Ouagadougou International Airport at 5:30 p.m.

I wanted to go welcome them at the airport, but there was no room in the pick-up truck for me since it was going to get all the American missionaries at the airport, as well as all their luggage and personal belongings. Instead of staying at home, I decided to walk from YFC to the airport. The distance between YFC and the airport was about nine miles. Even though it was a bit too far for me to walk, I so badly wanted to go welcome them. In our culture, it means a lot to go welcome somebody upon their arrival. I got to the airport a little before their arrival, so I waited with the other people who were waiting for them also. The Americans had traveled with Air France, and their flight number was 737; as soon as I heard the plane land, my heart rate started to speed up. I was more than anxious to see them.

As soon as they had everything checked through customs, I saw them coming toward the gate, and I immediately started looking for Joyce. As soon as I saw her coming, I ran into her arms and hugged her so hard, and she gave me a kiss on the cheek. While I was still hugging Joyce, a man came over and rubbed my hair. Immediately I knew it was Robert, and I gave him a hug too. I was very glad to see them again. I was so overwhelmed with joy that my hunger was gone that evening. The other people who were also at the airport came over and I greeted the group. I continued to stay by them, holding Joyce's hand as they waited for their suitcases. Once the team had received all of their luggage, my roommate Madi, who was once again their chauffer, started loading everything into the white pick-up truck. I started helping him load the stuff instead of just standing around and watching him. Once everything was loaded, there was no room in the pick-up truck for me to go with them to Wend and Celestine's house, which is where they were staying again. So, I said goodbye to Joyce and Robert and everyone else, and told them I'd meet them at Wend and Celestine's house.

I ran as fast as I could to meet them at the house. There were many people already gathered there to greet them, and most of them were youth. When I got there, I was tired and sweaty from running too far and too fast, but I pretended I was not tired so that no one would feel sorry for me. However, even though I pretended I was not tired, my clothes were wet and looked like I had taken a shower, which probably gave away my pretending. All of this didn't matter to me, though, because I was finally seeing the people I loved so dearly.

Not long after getting to the house, I began to help them unload all of their belongings. Once we finished unloading everything, some of the people started to leave so that the mission group could get some rest after their long trip. I didn't know whether I should leave or stay. Even though I wanted to stay longer, I felt like I should leave also since everyone else was leaving. I went inside the house to say good night to Joyce and Robert, and to welcome them again to Burkina-Faso. As soon as I told Joyce I was leaving, she asked me where I was going. I told her that I was going back to the YFC building, but she said, "No, no, no." She told me to sleep in their room on the floor by them instead of going back to the Youth for Christ center.

I wondered if I had misunderstood her or if she really wanted me to stay and sleep in their bedroom. So, I asked her, "Excuse me Joyce, I misunderstood you. Do you mean I can sleep in your bedroom tonight?"

"Yes," she replied.

I had nothing else to say but, "Okay, ma'am."

I went out and told Madi that Joyce had told me I could stay with them. I wanted to inform him that I would not be coming back that night, since we were roommates. By the time I got back to the bedroom, Joyce had already laid some blankets on the floor with some pillows on it for me to sleep on. I couldn't believe she was really doing this for me. After all, I was really sweaty and wet from running, and, I am sure I was stinking from wearing dirty clothes and not having had a shower for a while. Yet even after seeing how disgusting I was looking and smelling, she wanted me to sleep in the same room with them. That was unbelievable to me. I didn't know how to respond. I could see that she truly cared for and loved me. Though I was dirty, she wanted my company. Though I smelled bad, she wanted my hug. She cared about me inside and out, regardless of my appearance as a person. This is once again an example of the Jesus ministry. It is model of the true compassion Jesus Christ had for the lost and suffering. He, the son of God, stepped down from his highest, most glorious throne from heaven to dwell with people, to hang with us, to get dirty, to feel the rain, to be hungry, to know us on our most human level. In the same way, Joyce and Robert stepped down from their comfort zones, their nice heated and air-conditioned home and unlimited food supply, into the lives of people in need like myself. What an amazing love.

I slept really well that night. It was the first time I hadn't slept on a makeshift cardboard mattress on a hard cement floor, and I woke up fresh and well-rested in the morning. I asked Joyce and Robert how their night was, and they said it was great. They asked me how my night was, and I said it was good. I then went on to tell her how this was the first time I had slept on a soft place and not on the cement floor. I thanked them for letting me sleep in their room, and I told them how moved I felt by their caring heart towards me. We left the bedroom to go join everybody else in the living room. When we got there, there were all kinds of food waiting on the table. Wend and Celestine had a cook; he was the one who cooked their meals, as well as the American missionaries' meals. I was very hungry since I didn't have anything to eat the night before, but I was too shy to eat. I pretended that I wasn't really that hungry. After much convincing from everyone, I decided to take a little bit instead of a whole bunch, so that I would not look greedy and starving. I couldn't believe how much food the cook had fixed. I had never seen anything like that in all of my life.

I couldn't believe that I slept in the same house with

the Americans and had breakfast with them. In Burkina-Faso, being around and hanging out with "white" people is very respectable. Whenever a black person worked with white people, that person was highly respected by others. As for me, I was not only hanging out with them, but I was also sleeping and eating with them. This was surely a God thing. I went from being nobody to being somebody in the eyes of men and my peers.

After eating breakfast with the American missionaries, I left for school. They were getting ready to start the clinic for the day. Joyce gave me all kinds of candies and snacks, and she even gave me tennis shoes and some new clothes. I wore my new clothes and tennis shoes to school that day, and when I got there, some of the students didn't recognize me. They thought I was somebody else, because they had never seen me dressed that nicely. They were curious to know if I had won the lottery in order to buy my new things, but I kept telling them they came from God. The whole day I was very anxious for school to be over so I could go back "home" to be with the American missionaries—more specifically to be with Joyce and Robert, and to talk with them and get to know Robert better. I was not very focused that day at school. I thought of skipping class to be with the Americans, but I didn't because I didn't want Joyce and Robert to think that I was a bad student.

Soon after school was over, I went straight to see Joyce and Robert as well as the other Americans at Wend and Celestine's house. Upon my arrival, there were other people waiting to visit with them. I asked everyone how their day went, and how they liked

Burkina-Faso so far, since many on the team had never been there. Some said it was too hot for them, and others said they liked it. I told Joyce and Robert how my day had gone and what I had learned at school. Once again, the cook had dinner ready and it was waiting to be eaten. We sat down and had dinner together. After dinner was over, I helped the cook wash the dishes since there were too many dishes to wash for only one person. I felt so bad for him to be doing all the work by himself, and so I decided to help him.

Later on that evening, Franklin organized the group to have a time of worship before going to bed. We gathered around in the living room and sang songs, took prayer requests, prayed for each other, shared things with one another, and prayed for the days ahead in Burkina-Faso. Franklin, along with the other Americans, also spent time planning the next day, and some of the things that were on their agenda.

After we were done fellowshipping with one another, Joyce, Robert, Biba Foadley, Pastor Michel, and I met together to talk. Joyce and Robert had brought an airline ticket for me to go back with them to the United States! "Praise the Lord!" I yelled. I couldn't believe it. Although it was going to happen, it still seemed like a dream to me. Me going to the United States? Wow! What a great God I have, because I knew it had to be God who had made this happen.

I couldn't fall asleep that night. I was so overwhelmed with joy that I still can't find the words to express how I felt that night. I kept thanking God over and over through praise and worship. I couldn't believe that Joyce and Robert had done this for me. I didn't know how much the airline ticket had cost, but I knew it was expensive. Yet these people wanted me to go with them? The next day, we started to gather the different documents I needed for my trip to the United States. My life was about to turn around, for I knew clearly that God was moving me to another level, not just physically, but spiritually as well. I was more than excited to see the things he was about to do in my life.

PART THREE
FROM AFRICA
TO
AMERICA

6

PREPARING TO GO TO THE
UNITED STATES

*What he opens, no one can shut, and what he shuts, no one
can open.*
—Revelation 3:7

God was about to take me into a new level physically
and spiritually, but Satan was lying in wait to interrupt
his plan. However, I was prepared for this kind of
opposition. In the Bible, whenever God is about to do
something great, the enemy is also prepared to
counteract with his own tactics. God was about to
elevate me from a "nobody" to a "somebody," and I
knew that the enemy was going to try to fight back. My
preparing to go to the United States was the most intense
spiritual battle I have ever seen. Yet it was an amazing
opportunity to see the mighty hand of God at work.

On March 20, 1998, when I was seventeen, Robert,
Joyce, and I sat down to plan my trip. We were
scheduled to leave Africa two weeks from that day, and
gathering all the required documentation seemed to be
an almost insurmountable obstacle. It was definitely
going to take a miracle to make this all happen within
the time limits we faced. In addition to dealing with the
bureaucracy, it seemed as if everyone I knew—even
those that I had considered my close friends and

family—opposed the idea of me going to America with Joyce and Robert. I was surprised and hurt by their reactions, as until now they had always supported me and wanted the best for me. However, when an opportunity as wonderful as a trip to America presents itself, old tribal and family rivalries come out. I was born into the dominant Mossi tribe, but even those of my own tribe turned against me, because they wanted their own families, and not mine, to benefit from this chance. It was hard to experience this type of discrimination and racism within my own race and ethnic tribe; people saw me differently, because I belonged to the Tiendrebeogo family. More than just tribal and familial rivalries, though, the impoverished people of Burkina-Faso, like any other poor, hungry, and sick people, have a deep jealousy of anyone who gets a chance to rise above the poverty. It is understandable that everyone would want the chance to go to America for themselves—it was a rare gift. But I was still hurt by the way my friends turned against me.

Many people came to Robert and Joyce with accusations about me to make me look like a bad kid. Some people were saying that I was not a good Christian, while others were saying that I had bad friends and was getting into trouble. While everybody, including my friends and mentors, was against me, I learned that the Lord alone was my only hope and the one I could put my trust in, for he would never turn his back on me in times of trouble. As I was going through all those difficult accusations, I began to fast and pray continuously to the Lord Jesus more than ever before for his intervention. I prayed that since God had opened the door for me to go to the United States, no one else would be able to shut it. Despite all the allegations, accusations, and discriminations that were coming against me, I firmly believed what the Bible stated in Revelation 3:7, "What he opens, no one can shut, and what he shuts, no one can open." Therefore, there was no reason to be afraid. I knew that God was my father and that he was going to defend me.

One morning, I went to see Pastor Jean Tassembédo, a pastor who is known for intercession and prayer throughout the city. I went to see him so that we could pray together, because Matthew 18: 19-20 says: "For if two of you on earth agree about anything you ask for, it will be done for you by my Father in heaven. For where two or more come together in my name, there I am." Together with Pastor Jean, I began praying about getting all the documents we needed and for all the accusations and allegations that were coming against my trip to the United States to cease. He gave me the passage in Numbers 11:23 that states, "Is the hand of God too short?" He told me to believe and trust in God despite all the accusations and the short time we had to get all the documents. He then went on to explain to me that God is more than able to do what seems impossible in the eyes of men. Time after time we prayed together with regards to all the documents that I needed to have completed.

Despite all the lies that people were telling Robert and Joyce about me, they were still committed to taking me to the United States. They did not care what others had to say about me, but they decided to follow their hearts because they knew that God had told them to bring me to the United States. I wasn't really concerned or worried about Robert and Joyce changing their minds about taking me with them. Whether they were going to take me or not, I knew in my heart that if God said I was going to America, I would go no matter what the circumstances were—even if it was not going to be with Robert and Joyce. God had the final decision and there was no one in the heavens, on the earth, or beneath the earth that could challenge or interrupt his plans for my life.

Right from the beginning we needed God to intervene for us in order to get my passport in time. We knew we needed to gather many documents, but when we got the actual list from the Justice Department in Burkina-Faso, we were speechless. Two weeks was not long enough, but I had faith and believed that all things were possible through God. The prophet Jeremiah added that "nothing is too hard for him" (Jeremiah 32:17). Henry Blackaby and Richard Blackaby add that, "Words like 'cannot' and 'impossible' have no place in God's vocabulary. From heaven's perspective, nothing is impossible. Likewise, when God sets a plan in motion, failure is not an option." For that reason, I was not going to give up or worry—for I knew I was serving a miraculous God.

My roommate Madi drove Robert, Joyce, and me to all the different offices and departments we needed to go to in order to get the right documents. Madi and I also made an appointment to speak with a lady at the Justice Department, to see if she could give us assistance in getting the passport quickly. The normal length of time required to obtain a passport was at least two months, and we had less than two weeks.

One of the main papers we had to get was my certificate of nationality, which proved my citizenship of Burkina-Faso. In order to obtain that, I needed a signature from my mom or dad because I was under the age of eighteen. Due to the fact that my parents had both passed away, I needed another relative to sign the paper. The only other relative I had was François. He was still my legal guardian, so in order for me to go to the United States, he had to come to Ouagadougou to sign the papers. I was terrified when I learned this. The last time I had seen him he had tried to kill me, and four years had passed since then. Had his rage against me subsided, or did he still want to harm me? I had no idea how he was going to respond to the news that an American couple was taking me on a trip to America— perhaps he would refuse to sign the paper so that I couldn't go. Then there were the logistics of actually getting him to Ouagadougou to sign the document. I was so scared to ask him that I tried to find other people who could sign, but there was no one.

If I truly wanted to go to the United States, I had to let go of my fear and go back to the village and ask François to sign the document for me. Before going to the village, I went back and talked to Pastor Jean about the situation we were faced with and asked him to pray for me. Together, we prayed for my situation and at the end of our prayer, he told me to go back and talk to François and ask for forgiveness for everything that had happened in the past between the two of us. I didn't really know why I should go and ask for forgiveness because I had done nothing wrong. François was the one who had tried over and over to hurt me, and he even had attempted to take my life. Now Pastor Jean wanted me to go ask him for forgiveness? It wasn't making sense to me, but in the end, I agreed to do it. It was a way of avoiding conflict and dismantling the tension between us. Without forgiveness, it was impossible to reconnect as family members, and asking for forgiveness was the foundation. Together with Pastor Jean, we prayed that God would mold François' and my hearts to forgive each other and leave the past behind us. That night, I did nothing else but think about meeting with François and the uncertainty of not knowing what was going to happen.

The next day, Madi took Robert, Joyce, Francis, Biba, and me to the village with the YFC pickup truck. Upon our arrival to the village, everyone was at home, including François. Some were sitting under the huge tree that had a great amount of shade. They seemed very surprised to see me, but they were even more surprised to see me coming back with white people. In fact, I believe that it was a greater advantage for me that Robert and Joyce were white. After greeting each other, we explained why Robert and Joyce were there, and we told him about the passport situation and that we needed to have him go to Ouagadougou to sign the papers for me. François argued over and over about how disrespectful I had been to him and the entire family. Yet, despite everything he was saying about me, my job was simply to say "I am sorry" over and over, and not try to defend myself. I was listening to everything he was saying and not arguing with him because arguing with him would just make things worse. It was very hard for me to tell him I was sorry when he was the one who tried to kill me, but my reason for going and apologizing was not to try to debate who was right and who was wrong. Our mission was to reconcile with him and the entire family. After a long two hours of talking with him and asking for forgiveness, he finally agreed to go to Ouagadougou with us to sign the certificate of nationality. What a major answer to prayer! I was overjoyed that he was willing to sign the paper for me and let me go to America. He was very happy for what Robert and Joyce were doing for me, and he even gave them two big chickens—a common way to say thank you in Burkina-Faso.

Once we were all done talking, François followed us to Ouagadougou on his motorbike to sign the paper. Upon our arrival into the city, we went straight to the Justice Department and François signed the paper. After he had signed it, we gave him some food and found a place for him to sleep so that he would not have to drive home that night. Robert and Joyce gave him some money to buy two bags of rice for the family as a way of showing our appreciation for what he did for me. The next day he rode his motorbike back to the village.

Through the process of going back to François, God taught me the power behind the phrase "I am sorry." This very powerful phrase penetrates deep in the heart and dismantles all arguments, all wrongs, and all offenses. Saying "I am sorry" is very simple, yet so powerful that it destroys the tactics of the enemy. Once one says "I am sorry," the other person has only to forgive and move on. I understood the reason why Pastor Jean had told me to go ask François for forgiveness.

After the paper was signed, we were able to get the rest of the necessary papers for the passport. Thanks to a Christian woman who worked in the Justice Department, but most of all, God Almighty, the process was done in about one week instead of the normal time. We all took the time to thank God for his favor and help in getting the passport.

There were not words to express my thankfulness to God for all the ways he intervened in the process of getting the passport. In my lack of faith, I could not believe that we could obtain the passport in one week. God brought all the right people at the right time, and even François was willing to come and help, when I thought he would want nothing to do with me. Not only was he willing to help, he was even happy for me! My roommate Madi was also a blessing to me. He was willing to take us on all the many trips we needed to take in order to get the different papers we needed, and he did it without complaining. Joyce even wrote in her journal from the trip, "If it wasn't for Madi, we would probably have dropped it all. He was willing to do all the legwork and paperwork, and he wanted to see Jean-Paul go to America so badly."

After receiving the passport, Pastor Jean and I fasted and thanked God for his favor, and for shaming the people who were against me. However, the passport was only one of the necessary items that I needed in order to get to America. I also needed my visa, which Pastor Jean and I began to pray for, and that the Lord would give us favor for the consular that we were about to face. Once again we had to rely on God and trust that he would speak for us.

On March 26, four days before we received my passport, Robert and Joyce officially started the process to get my visa. On that day, they went to the United States Embassy and met with a lady for an interview. During their meeting, Barbra told Robert and Joyce that they needed to supply her with sufficient evidence to prove that I was going to return to Burkina-Faso. As a way of showing her that I was going to return to the country, Robert and Joyce purchased a piece of land to start building a home on it during my visit in the United States. Purchasing this land was enough evidence to prove to the United States Embassy that I had a reason to return to the country.

On April 1, we went to the American Embassy and got an application for the visa. One of the requirements for obtaining the visa was a parental letter giving me permission to go to the United States. Once again, François was the only one who could do this for me. So, Madi and I went back to the village and picked up François and brought him back to Ouagadougou. François didn't know how to write, so we had to take him to the secretarial office to have them type what he said. We then took the letter to the national police station where they re-wrote the letter, stamped and notarized it, and then had François sign it.

After we had the letter from François completed, we took the letter, visa application, and the forty-five dollar fee to the embassy. Upon our arrival, we gave them my application and my passport, and were told to come back the same day at four o'clock in the afternoon. I wondered if there was a problem with our application that we had to come back later, but we had no other choice but to follow their instructions.

While waiting, we went to the American club to eat lunch, but I couldn't really eat because I was so anxious about what was going to happen. After waiting for what seemed like forever, four o'clock finally arrived. Robert, Joyce, and I walked to the embassy from the American Club Center. Upon our arrival, Barbra handed my passport with the visa stamped inside to Robert and said, "Have safe traveling!" I didn't know exactly what that meant, but I knew I was officially on my way to America! Together, we walked away from the embassy, laughing and slapping hands. We then walked back to the American Club, and when we got there, everyone yelled and hollered in excitement with us.

By the mighty favor of God, I was able to obtain my passport and visa in a matter of thirteen days, and was on my way to America. Despite all the allegations and other various oppositions, the Lord had given us total victory in the presence of those who were against me. As King David sang and praised the Lord in 2 Samuel 21:2, as he was delivered from the hand of his enemies, I too sang and praised the Lord. I said to the Lord, you are "my rock, my fortress and my deliverer." I was very thankful to the Lord not only for the opportunity to go to the United States, but also for teaching me that nothing was impossible with him. Although I knew I was really going to go to the United States, it still seemed like a dream. I could not wait to discover America. All my life I had heard stories from people about the beauty of the United States. I was finally going to get the chance to discover it with my own eyes, and I was only seventeen years old.

On the night of April 5, we were getting ready to leave Burkina-Faso. Many people came and said goodbye to us at the airport, including those who were originally against me going to the United States, but now appeared to be very excited for me. As I was saying goodbye to my friends and all that I knew, I was also saying goodbye to poverty and hunger for I knew I was going to a place where there was no pain, crying, hunger or poverty—a place where milk and honey are free for all, a place of hope and happiness. I was very anxious to get out of Burkina-Faso for the United States, and I could not wait to fly in a plane and feel it for myself. I wondered what the inside of the plane looked like.

At eleven o'clock at night, we boarded the plane and were headed to Paris, France, for our first layover. It was such a great feeling to see the lights over the country. However, I was somewhat scared as the plane was bouncing back and forth and I wondered if it was going to crash. I held Joyce's hand firmly the whole way and never let go until the plane was settled. The number of white people aboard the plane greatly outnumbered the number of black people. I thought to myself that the black people were probably rich, with the exception of me.

While I was on my way to the United States I thought so much about the grace and love of God for me. I was deeply into the presence of Lord as the Holy Spirit was talking to me about his love and grace for me. I was living in his grace, which was far beyond my own comprehension and understanding. After all, I am sure that Robert and Joyce saw many people in Burkina-Faso who were just as much in need as I was, but for some reason they chose me. I am sure they saw many people who were either abandoned by their families or had lost their parents. Yet, they chose me over the thousands of suffering, poor people that they saw. I kept asking the Lord, "Why me, Lord? Why me?" Who was I to be going to the United States? My whole life, as I was shepherding the animals, running away from François, washing dishes and doing all kinds of dirty work, and sleeping on cardboard, I was a nobody. Who was I to be riding in plane full of rich white people? There was nothing I could do and no words to express my appreciation to God for his grace and favor on my life. The only words on my lips were, "Thank you Lord; thank you Lord." What an amazing grace.

I slept a lot on our way from Burkina-Faso to Paris, and when we got to Paris, we had a little bit of a problem with me not having a French visa, but they let me through, thanks to the great favor of God. We eventually got on our connecting flight to Toronto, Canada, and after nine and a half hours of traveling, we finally arrived in Toronto. As we were about to board the plane to the United States, an immigration officer came and checked everyone's passports. When we were inside the terminal, a Canadian immigration officer stopped us because I did not have a Canadian visa. They wanted to deport me from Toronto back to Burkina-Faso. Although I did not have a visa to Canada, I put the whole situation in the hands of God and pleaded with him to be my defender. After a series of questions and a long delay, they let us go through because Robert and Joyce were American citizens. From Toronto, we flew into Columbus, Ohio, and then into Dayton, Ohio. Once we reached the Dayton

International Airport, Robert and Joyce's family was there to welcome us to the United States and to take us back to Robert and Joyce's house in Waynesfield, Ohio.

At the end of our journey, I was thankful to be done. After all the work and anticipation, I was finally in America! I reflected back on this great change in my life, and what it was that led Robert and Joyce to notice me and want to bring me back to their home. When I asked Joyce, she said:

> I didn't really know what to expect when I went to Burkina-Faso in 1997. The heat from the weather as I stepped off the plane, the stern looks from the customs people, the crowd of people there to greet us, as well as the red dust. All that was soon forgotten as I got to know the people and see the joy on their faces as we did such small things for them. The appreciation they expressed touched me. The second or third day we were there and loading into the back of an old pick-up truck, a small boy was there in his very ragged clothes wanting to go with us to the village we were going to and he was allowed to go with us several times. He came to where we where staying one evening and had peanuts tied in individual packets for each of us. We were all so touched because we knew he surely didn't have enough to eat himself and he gave us some peanuts. Of course I took his address back to America with me and the year I went back to Burkina-Faso with a husband, I was anxious to see Jean-Paul again and soon started pursuing a way to take this boy to America with us for a visit. The Lord answered a lot of prayers and made it possible and I felt like I

*had become a mother all over again. Jean-Paul clung
to me and depended on me. Something I needed at
this time in my life and he fulfilled my needs as I tried
to fill the void in his life of a mother's touch.*

Without a doubt, God hears the cries of his children.
The cries of my heart rose up to him and he
miraculously sent Robert and Joyce from the United
States to Africa to rescue me from all my sufferings—the
suffering of loneliness, feeling unwanted, rejection, and
of course hunger. Being where I was, I thought that I
needed Robert and Joyce desperately in my life to help
me with my various needs. I didn't think they needed
me since it appeared that they had everything they
needed. Surprisingly, I was about to find out that God
was about to use me to fill the void in their hearts, while
at the same time using them to show his unfailing,
unconditional love to me.

MAP SHOWING THE LOCATION OF BURKINA-FASO

HOUSES THAT I GREW UP IN, WHICH ARE MADE OF MUD BRICKS

WOMEN AND CHILDREN LINED UP WITH THEIR CONTAINERS WAITING FOR WATER

THIS IS THE SCHOOL I ATTENDED WHEN I WAS LIVING IN THE VILLAGE

THESE ARE SOME OF THE ORPHANS THAT IDRISSA
AND HIS WIFE TAKE CARE OF

THIS IS THE "NERE" TREE WHERE CHURCH SERVICES
WERE HELD

THIS IS A PICTURE OF ME IN MY ROOM AT YFC. ON
THE WALL WERE THE CLOTHES I HAD AND
ON THE LEFT SIDE WAS MY BED.

JOYCE WATCHING ME GOING THROUGH SOME OF MY
BELONGINGS IN MY BEDROOM AT YFC.

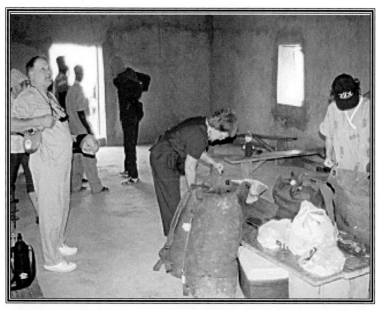

THE AMERICANS MISSIONARIES GOING THROUGH SOME OF THE BAGS LOADED WITH MEDICINE.

THE AMERICAN MISSIONARIES RIDING IN THE YFC PICK-UP TRUCK TRAVELING TO GO TREAT PEOPLE. I AM THE ONE SITTING IN THE MIDDLE WITH THE HAT ON.

PEOPLE WAITING TO BE TREATED BY THE AMERICAN MISSIONARIES AT A CHURCH.

MORE PEOPLE WAITING TO BE TREATED BY THE AMERICAN MISSIONARIES AT A NEARBY CHURCH.

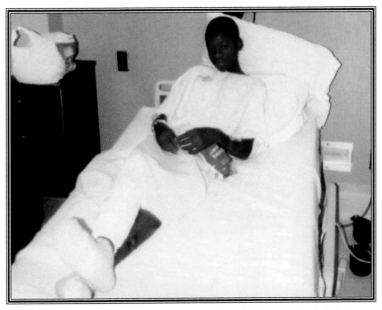

PICTURE OF ME LAYING ON THE BED AT THE HOSPITAL AFTER SURGERY.

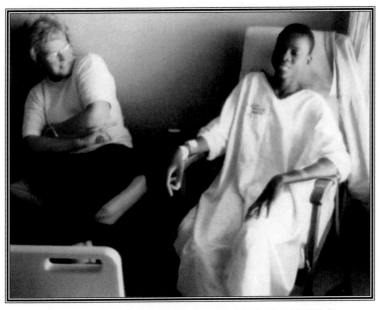

MOM AND I CHATTING AT THE HOSPITAL AFTER SURGERY.

7

DISCOVERING A WHOLE "NEW WORLD"

*However, the Lord your God would not listen to Balaam
but turned the curse into a blessing for you, because the
Lord your God loves you.*
—Deuteronomy 23:5

On my way to Robert and Joyce's home from the
airport, I was amazed at the beauty of Ohio. All of the
lights from the city made the night-time seem like
daytime. Unlike the streets in Burkina-Faso, the roads
were clean, and surprisingly, there were no bicycles,
motorbikes, donkeys, or people walking on the roads.
Instead, the road was full of beautiful cars and trucks
traveling at very fast speeds. I kept looking left and
right so that I wouldn't miss anything around me. There
were no words to express how I felt. All was beautiful as
I expected. When we finally arrived home, I was
amazed at the house that Robert and Joyce own. A "nice
little heaven" full of everything one could need and
beautiful cars parked in the garage. I spent a couple of
hours just observing everything—the house, the cars,
everything. I was so overwhelmed with the experience
that when Joyce asked me if I wanted something to eat I
said no, even though I was hungry.

Later on that night, Joyce took me to the bedroom I

was going to stay in upstairs. Instead of falling asleep right away, I spent a long time looking at everything that I had never seen before. I praised God that night with all of my heart for blessing me beyond what I could have dreamed. From Africa, he brought me to the United States; from a nobody, he made me a somebody; from not having anyone, he gave me a family; and from sleeping on a hard, cement floor, I was about to be sleeping on a nice, soft bed. Wow! God is really an amazing God. Somewhere in the midst of gazing at everything, I fell asleep. I had peace in my inner being and I knew that I was in a safe place. I slept well that night, and I didn't wake up until later the next day.

When I finally got up, Robert and Joyce decided to take me to their family doctor, Dr. Cummings, to have her look at my infected leg. After living with the infection for so long, I had become so used to the pain that I barely noticed it. However, it was so infected that I was afraid it was going to have to be amputated. While I was in Africa, I tried to keep it clean, but there were no bandages or anything to put on it. I had mixed feelings about going in to see the doctor, not knowing what was going to happen, but I prayed to God that he would watch over me and take care of me. When we arrived at Dr. Cummings' office, she inspected my leg for several minutes and asked me a few questions. In the end, she decided to contact another doctor to take a look at it—Dr. Ellis, who was an infectious disease specialist. She made an appointment for Dr. Ellis to see me the next day.

The next day, April 9, we went to Dr. Ellis' office. He inspected my leg and asked me several questions about the history of my health. At the end of our visit, he decided to send us to Lima Memorial Hospital for surgery. We went straight to the hospital and were placed in the room where the surgery was to take place. After waiting the whole day for Dr. Ellis, he finally showed up at eleven p. m. for the surgery. He gave me some pain medication, which put me to sleep before the surgery started. Having pain medication was something totally new to me, because in Burkina-Faso, most people never receive pain reliever, but instead just suffer. Living with pain and suffering is the way of life. According to Robert and Joyce, Dr. Ellis opened my leg up and washed it out with some antiseptics. The surgery lasted an hour. I didn't have a clue how much the surgery was going to cost Robert and Joyce. In Burkina-Faso, we can go to the hospital with four or five dollars, but I knew this was not the case in the United States. I didn't want Robert and Joyce to spend all their money on my leg. At the end of the surgery, for whatever reason, Dr. Ellis decided not to charge them anything. He did it from the goodness of his heart. I thanked Dr. Ellis very much and kept praising God for his miracles.

I stayed at the hospital overnight, and the next day Dr. Ellis came at noon and changed the bandages before sending us home. I was not allowed to put a lot of pressure on that leg, but I was not in a wheelchair or on crutches. I was so thankful that Dr. Ellis was able to fix my leg without amputating it. I also could not believe that for the first time, my leg was starting to experience some healing. I was overjoyed to have my leg back because many times I hadn't been able to do certain things because of the infection and pain.

During my one-and-a-half day stay at the hospital, I

experienced the difference between being a patient in an American hospital versus an African hospital. I was amazed by how Dr. Cummins and Dr. Ellis treated their patients compared to the way doctors in Burkina-Faso treat their patients. Here, they have all the high technologies, while in Burkina-Faso the doctors barely have anything to use on their patients. Here, they care first for the patient and take care of the bills later, while in Africa, you have to pay the doctors cash before they will see you. Moreover, in the United States, there are nurses and other persons that care for patients, while in Africa, patients are left alone with their family members, waiting for hours or even days for a doctor or nurse to show up to treat them. Sadly, the rich patients are always the ones that the doctors and nurses see first, while the poor are lying on their beds waiting to die. According to many, doctors in Burkina-Faso get two paychecks every month—one from the corruption of the rich person's bribes, and the second as their normal salary at the end of every month.

On our way home from the hospital, Robert and Joyce stopped at K-Mart to get me some necessities. I was surprised by how big the store was and the fact that one could find everything in it. I was speechless. Unlike our markets in Burkina-Faso, this one had everything—clothes, shoes, bikes, food, a pharmacy, and much more. I kept staring at everyone and everything. What a cool market, I thought. Yet Robert and Joyce told me that it was nothing compared to the shopping malls. They later took me to go see the Lima Mall, which was far beyond what I had ever thought possible. Unlike our stores that are dirty, their stores are clean, orderly with everything placed properly, and it was easy to find things with people available to help whenever needed. The downside is that there was no price negotiation. Either you buy it for its marked price or leave it. In the African markets, the merchants will do everything to convince you to buy their products; it was a different experience for me to purchase things without a merchant pressuring me to buy his goods. Even more amazing to me was that I could even return my product to the store here if I did not like it or if there was some problem with it. That is unheard of in African markets.

Robert and Joyce bought me three pairs of pants and three shirts that day at K-Mart. We also bought a pair of shoes. When I got home, I got on my knees and thanked God for all his blessings. For years, I had been sleeping and waking up with the same clothes everyday, and now I had clothes to change into and stay clean. I was getting a total makeover.

Dr. Ellis continued to monitor the progress of my leg during my stay in the United States. Robert, Joyce, and I made many trips to his office for consultations and for him to check my leg. I had to clean it with some peroxide and other medications three times a day. While my leg was healing, Robert and Joyce feared that I was bored being at home too much. They decided to contact the principal of Waynesfield Goshen High School, Kathy Lament, and ask her if it was possible for me to attend classes there for the remainder of the school year. After thinking deeply about Robert and Joyce's request, Ms. Lament accepted their request and granted me her permission to enroll in Art, English, and American History.

I was very pleased that I was able to start going to school again. I have always enjoyed learning about new things in the classroom. Since I was the only black student in my classes, my goal was to earn respect from the American students and teachers. I knew I could do that through my academic performance and my lifestyle. Even though my English compared to many Burkinabè was very good, in the United States it still needed a lot of work. However, with a positive attitude and hard work I overcame that weakness. Being able to go to school in Waynesfield was an opportunity I had never thought I would have. I wanted to do well and make Robert and Joyce happy and proud of my academic performance.

It was very interesting to see the classroom setting and atmosphere in the United States compared to Africa. In the United States, there are only a few students in the classroom, while in Africa, the classroom is packed with sixty to seventy students, making it impossible for one teacher to handle everyone. In Africa, we respect our teachers greatly, while in the United States, some of the students don't know how to show respect at all. At times it was like the teacher was a student because the students were not treating the teacher any differently than their classmates. I was amazed that education was free to everyone in the United States from first grade to high school. I was also surprised that there were buses to transport all the students back and forth to school everyday. In Africa, everyone has to walk to school. Only the rich children have bicycles or motorbikes to travel with. In fact, some of the teachers even walk since they don't get paid enough to afford a motorbike. Out of all these things, what shocked me the most were the times reserved for lunch for all the students. In Burkina-Faso, only few could afford to eat lunch, making it hard for the rest of us to listen to or see what the teacher had to say or show; a hungry person doesn't have a listening ears or seeing eyes.

As I started attending the classes, I was surprised by the warm welcome I received from the students and teachers. They were all staring at me, and at first I wondered why. Was it because I was black or different from them? After a while it didn't bother me too much, so I ignored them and went on with school. Some of them were very friendly to me, and they all had questions about Africa. They were curious to know what Africa was like and what kind of animals we had there. It was clear to me that most Americans knew nothing about Africa, except that the continent is home to many wild animals. I wondered what they were learning in the classroom about Africa. I quickly recognized that we were all blind to each other's way of life. Instead, we tend to assume things. I tried to answer most of their questions so that they could truly learn something about African culture.

In the classroom, I learned a lot about the United States—its history, its journey to freedom, its people, and its constitution. Unlike the Burkina-Faso constitution, which people change day to day to fit their personal motives, the United States' is unchangeable; its government is elected of the people by the people, for the people. Furthermore, being in the classroom greatly helped improve my verbal and written English. I discovered that total immersion in a new culture is the best way to learn a language.

Because I was not enrolled as a full-time student at the high school, I had some time before and after my classes. During that time, I would help Robert with his work and whatever he was doing. Even though he was retired, he was still active and always had something to do. Though my leg was not fully healed, I was devoted to assisting him, as he and Joyce had blessed me greatly. Every time I saw Robert or Joyce doing some kind of work, I would go along and help them even if they didn't ask me to help. Joyce always had something to do. Whether it was working on the farm, planting flowers, pulling weeds, cooking, or cross-stitching, she was always busy with something. They were like a dad and mom to me and I wanted to help them instead of sitting down and doing nothing. Day after day, Robert and I spent time working on different construction projects. Though Robert was not a construction worker by profession, he had most of the tools he needed in order to complete many projects in a short amount of time. In Africa, everything is done by hand because we lack the technology and machinery needed to do jobs quickly. Africa will likely lag far behind the Western world until there is better access to technology. Within a matter of two months or so, we were able to complete far beyond what I would have thought or imagined.

In addition to helping Robert with construction, I was also helping on the farm and around the house. I learned how hard American farmers work—they are the last ones to go to bed at night and the first ones to get up in the morning. I learned how to bale hay with the tractors, feed the cows, and I even went to their county fair to watch others show steer. I was helping Robert and Joyce to show my appreciation to them, but also to show them and everybody else how hard Africans work. I wanted to be a role model, a good example, and a representative of African people to them. I wanted to show them that we Africans have the hearts of hard workers so that they would not get the impression that we are just lazy people sitting around seeking help from others. Thankfully, the tools they had made the work go a lot faster. My history teacher in Burkina-Faso once told us in class that a single American farmer is able to provide enough food for the entire country of Burkina-Faso. We thought he was lying, but during my time in the United States, I saw that his statement was true.

When school was over and my leg had improved, Robert and Joyce decided to take me around the country so that I could see other parts of the United States. During the month of June, we flew to Tucson, Arizona, to visit Robert's brother Lee and his wife, Sally. I didn't know how diverse the United States was until I got to Arizona. It was interesting to see different climates, different temperatures, different houses, and even different cultures within the same country. Upon our arrival, Lee and Sally took us around Tucson. While we were in Arizona, we also went and visited the Grand Canyon. I was amazed by what I saw, and I kept asking questions about how the Grand Canyon came to exist. Robert and Joyce, as well as Lee and his wife, tried to answer some of my questions, yet, the more questions they answered, the more questions I had. I kept gazing at it, and I was amazed by its width, depth, and range.

The more I looked at it, the more I contemplated God's amazing wonders—his mighty power and amazing creation. It made me realize how powerful and majestic is the God we serve. My heart grew even more fearful and reverent toward God.

After our visit to the Grand Canyon, Robert and Joyce bought a motor home. It was a nice motor home that had everything that a regular house had in it. Seeing a motor home for the first time and living in it for several days was quite an adventure for me. I couldn't believe it was an entire house on wheels. It had a shower, kitchen, bed, restroom and even a television. I was speechless. We drove it from Arizona all the way back to Ohio. On our way back, I discovered many other parts of the United States. I was blessed to get an opportunity to see so much, including the states of Texas, Oklahoma, Arkansas, Tennessee and Kentucky. Once again, I was amazed by the differences I saw within every state. Robert and Joyce made many stops in those states to show me important sites. They wanted me to see as much of the United States as possible before returning to Africa. It was unreal to see the uniqueness of every state, and I realized just how big the United States really is.

When we returned home, we rested for a couple of days before embarking on yet another journey. This time, we decided to go to Port Huron, Michigan, for me to visit Franklin Spotts and his family. When we got there, I stayed with Franklin for two days while Robert and Joyce were camping in their new motor home in a nearby park. Franklin took me and showed me the city of Port Huron. We also visited several churches and a local school where Franklin's son Andre was a school teacher. Wherever we went, Franklin wanted me to share my testimony with people, something that was really hard for me to do. I felt like I was re-living the past every time I shared my testimony with other people. I also helped Franklin make some booklets entitled "The Biblical God Reaching His Creation," for him to bring to Africa on his next trip. I was very surprised by Franklin's lifestyle. He was living simply, wearing the same clothes over and over. I admire his heart and dedication to spreading the gospel of Jesus Christ, not only in Africa, but even here in the United States. At the end of my visit with Franklin, Robert, Joyce, and I returned to Waynesfield. Like in our previous trip, we made several stops to see different sites and explore the beauty of Michigan. Mackinac Island was one of many sites I was able to visit during our short trip to Michigan.

By the time we got back from visiting Franklin, my journey to the United States was coming to an end. After spending three months with Robert, Joyce, and their family members and friends, my relationship with them was filial. I no longer saw them only as my friends, but as my parents. In fact, I had started calling them "Mom" and "Dad." They were my new family that God had given me, and they had treated me like I was their very own son. I even began to develop a relationship with their children and grandchildren. I was very moved by Robert and Joyce's generosity and love for me. During my time in the United States, they ministered to me by feeding me, clothing me, and parenting me. Joyce (Mom) loved to cook for people, and every day there was food already prepared for me before I even got out of bed. She was always making sure that I was well fed, and she even gave me snacks throughout the day. I remember one time she told me that in America, you do not wait to get hungry, you eat before you get hungry. This was something that was incomprehensible to me because the women in the village withheld food from me even when there was enough for everyone, despite all the chores I did for them. More than that, every time we went to a store or the mall, I always came back with something new. I always came home either with clothes, food, or something else. My first three months in America were vastly different than my first sixteen years in Africa! Within a matter of three months I grew four inches taller. However, despite all the food that I ate, I did not gain any weight at all.

I was very blessed by Dad and Mom's love and compassion for me. I could not understand why my own flesh and blood in Burkina-Faso did not want me, yet this couple just found me in Africa and was now treating me like their very own. They even told me on several occasions that they loved me as they loved their own children. On one occasion I received a card from Dad and Mom that read, "Son, you have a forever place in our heart, where every happy memory, proud moment, and joy you've brought to life is tucked away with love." Those words penetrated deep into my heart and would not let go. It was a love that I had not known from any human for a very long time. I now had people who cared for me, who would hug me and show me affection, who would cry with me and hold my hand when I needed comfort, who would tell me that I was loved—this is what I had been searching and longing for since the day my mother died. Although I had been blessed with several brothers and sisters in Christ in Africa, my relationship with Dad and Mom transcended all other relationships. I now belonged with someone. Not only did they show me the emotional love that I needed, but they also provided for my physical needs. They took me to the doctor right away for my infected leg, while Tinkoudgou and François spent years ignoring it, and instead wasted their money on alcohol and other unnecessary things. Why was it that I had to go all the way to the United States to find the love and acceptance and basic care that I never could find in Africa?

Throughout my journey in the United States, I grew even more aware of the vast differences between Africa and the United States. I wondered why the United States was so very different in comparison to Burkina-Faso. It was like heaven versus hell or black versus white. I wondered why Americans had everything in abundance while millions of Africans lack the basic necessities such as food to eat, clear water to drink, or even a shelter to lay their heads at night. While American farmers feed their cows with corn and beans, millions of Africans are starving. While Americans shop for groceries for their dogs and the birds, many in Africa can't even have the minimum proteins their body needs. The disparity caused me to wonder why God had blessed America and not Africa.

It is very difficult for starving, sick people to see God in the midst of their suffering; though many people on the African continent confess to loving God, many people wonder about the sincerity of God's love or his promises to his people. The reality of God's grace is frequently questioned there. After experiencing the overabundance of America, I also questioned why God allowed starvation and suffering to be part of the daily lives of the world's poor. Had we done something to anger him? I was frustrated for my inability to answer those questions. Later on, I grew to understand that many of the problems in Africa were not allowed by God, but rather were a result of corrupt men and ethnic strife. This dynamic can't be well understood in the United States, since, for the most part, different ethnicities and religions are accepted and even celebrated. Though racial tensions do exist, the level of hatred that the ethnic tribes of Africa often have for each other is rarely seen in America, while it is a part of everyday life in Africa.

The more I thought about going back, the more sadness would envelop me. I didn't want to return to Burkina-Faso. I feared that I would go back just to end up in the same type of misery that I was in before coming to the United States. I had become used to living with a family and now I was about to return home to the loneliness that waited for me there. I was so sad about leaving that at times I refused to eat or talk to Robert and Joyce. I hoped that they would change their minds and have me stay with them forever, but I learned that crying, sulking, or refusing food wasn't going to make that happen. Though I knew God had a great plan for my life, I was worried about my future. I knew that Robert and Joyce wanted me to stay longer with them and they were all sad that I was about to return home, but we all wanted to be faithful and keep our promise to the United States embassy about me returning to Burkina-Faso. I remember crying so hard when the day came for me to return home. I cried and cried while holding on to Joyce's hands very tight, not wanting to let her go. I cried so much that my eyes became big like the ones of an eagle. I didn't want to go back, but I didn't have a choice.

8

RETURNING TO AFRICA

Wealth brings many friends, but a poor man's best friend deserts him.
—Proverbs 19:4

My physical appearance was much different when I returned to Burkina-Faso than it had been when I left. Not only was I significantly taller, I was no longer dirty and I did not have the tired, hungry look of a homeless child. I soon gained the nickname "Americain," which translates into "American," because of my trip. I stood out now from the others because I had nice new clothes, shoes, and other belongings. I also found that I had suddenly left behind the social outcast "YFC boy" stigma and had joined—at least socially—the upper middle class. I was now a "somebody."

I quickly learned that most of my new "friends" only sought me out because they wanted my help. Most Burkinabè are convinced that the United States is a place where money is all over the place and everybody is rich and has everything they could ever want. Many of them wanted me to try to use my connections to get them a trip to America. This phenomenon was something I had witnessed before when people had returned to Burkina-Faso from the United States, but I never understood the extent of it until I was the "lucky" one. I felt like a Hollywood star. Even those "enemies" who had tried to sabotage my trip to America and the "rich" children who never had wanted to associate with me now wanted to be my friends. Before going to America, no one really listened to me, but now when I spoke, people listened. I had more friends than ever before in my life. There is an African proverb that states, "When you have money, you have friends, but when you are poor, you have no one." Sadly, this proverb proved to be the reality of how people, including Christians, chose to treat me. Although it was a struggle—my new popularity made me feel important and it was sometimes hard to remember that it was really just a façade—I knew who my true friends were. The people who were my friends when I had nothing, who were my friends even when I was an outcast, who shared their lunches with me when I was dizzy and sick from hunger—those were my true friends.

Regardless of their motivations for seeking me out, everyone was curious about America. I showed many people the pictures I had taken while I was in the United States, and we talked about the differences between American culture and our own. I explained to them how American people were busy, and how time was precious to them. I once heard as a child that "time was money" in America, and I had witnessed this to be true. While I was in the States, it appeared to me that people's lives were being run by the clock. It was as if they were slaves of time, which made it very hard to find time to talk with them. Everybody was busy trying to finish their agenda before sunset, and millions even work at night. In Burkina-Faso, time is not a concern in comparison to relationships with people.

Everyone was amazed when I told them that many Americans had one, two, or even three different cars to drive around, and how hard it was to find our way home when we would get lost. This was so different from Burkina-Faso, because when one gets lost, there are always people on the street to ask for help. In America, one must be able to read the signs. I told them about the busy highways and about the huge malls and shopping centers, and how one can go into a shopping center and buy everything he or she could possibly want. I also told and showed them the kinds of houses people lived in, and how everyone lived in a two-or three-story high house. I also shared about Robert and Joyce's church service. It was short and straight to the point. In Burkina-Faso we would spend three to four hours in church, singing, dancing, and praying. Burkinabè, though they are poor and have nothing to do, are free and open to long church services compared to Americans, who are bound by time and their daily agendas. And yes, I told them how rich Americans were—how everybody considered themselves as "middle-class" people, but yet are not satisfied to be in the middle-class. I even told them about the fast food system that exists in America and how Americans seem to eat all the time. I told them how surprised I was to see that some Americans feed their animals with the same kind of food people eat in Burkina-Faso, and I told them that American pets, such as dogs and cats, are fed better than most Burkinabè. In short, I told them what my eyes saw America as—a beautiful, rich country, a new world that was very different than ours. Indeed, it was a place full of hope and happiness. Even if all of my views were not completely accurate, that was what I saw with my eyes in the short time that I was there.

Most people I spoke with assumed that because I had been to this land of abundance that I had brought some of it home with me. People thought that I had a lot of money and many of them—some of whom I had never met before—came and explained their problems to me with the hope that I could do something for them. I spent a lot of time talking with people and listening to their problems. I knew in my heart that they needed more than just their physical needs met, and that a trip to America was not going to give them the fulfillment they desired. While their physical needs were obvious, they needed more than earthly food and money. Most of them carried an incredible amount of pain, frustration, and anger. What they needed was a savior, and since I had that savior in me, it was an opportunity for me to preach the gospel. It became an opportunity for me to introduce them to the one who could help them, for I knew that I could not. God was the only one who had taken me out of the situation I was in at one time.

I used this opportunity to introduce them to Jesus Christ, and my trip to America was a catalyst for me to reach out to my people. Many people came to me and told me their stories, problems, and needs, and I usually listened to them. In the end, I always told them about the one who helped me with my problems and the one who took me to America. God was all they needed, because once they met him, he was more than able to deliver them from their horrible living conditions. Because I preached to many people, I gained the nickname of "Pastor Jean-Paul" or "mad boy," and

wherever I went people referred to me by those
nicknames. I wasn't bothered or concerned by those
nicknames because I knew what I was doing. In fact, I
am glad that I gained those nicknames for the sake of
the gospel more than any other reason.

Although I welcomed the opportunity to share Christ
with others, I was overwhelmed by the number of
people who were coming to me for help. They were
indeed in great need and I knew that they needed some
kind of physical and financial assistance, but I didn't
come home from America with tons of money like
people thought I did. Nonetheless, with the little money
that was given to me, I tried to help the people that I
could. I just didn't have enough to help the whole
country, and I still had to make sure that I had what I
needed to survive. My heart was troubled—I knew that
God was the only one that could truly heal these people.
In Acts 3:2-6, Peter says to a crippled man, "Silver and
gold I do not have to give you. In the name of Jesus
Christ of Nazareth, walk." However, I also knew that
these people needed to have their basic physical needs
met. James 2:15-16 states: "Suppose a brother or sister is
without clothes and daily food. If one of you says to
him, 'Go, I wish you well, keep warm and well fed,' but
does nothing about his physical needs, what good is it?"
I was sharing the gospel with the people of my country,
but in the meantime they were starving, sick, and
destitute. In Africa, we have a proverb that states, "An
empty stomach does not listen." This proverb is very
true. Most people I spoke with were not interested in
what I had to say. They were concerned with their
immediate needs and not their eternal needs. I know

from experience—getting through "today" is more pressing than worrying about "tomorrow" for someone who is starving. It became very clear to me that Third World ministries could be far more effective if they would provide for both the physical and spiritual needs of the people.

After experiencing the generosity of Robert and Joyce, the reality that poor people will go to extremes to provide for themselves came crashing down on me shortly after my return to Burkina Faso. I learned after going home that my house, which Mom and Dad had been sending money to build, was not built at all—even though the person in charge had told us that everything was done and ready prior to my arrival. I was very surprised and disappointed. I had anticipated finally having my own house, but I found myself once again homeless. Not only was the house not built, but the money that Mom and Dad had sent over for the house was gone. I also found out that the person who was supposed to build the house for me had sold the land Robert and Joyce had purchased prior to my trip to America to another person. My heart was broken by this deception.

The person we sent the money to for the house used it and bought himself some goods, including a motorbike. I could not understand why he had done what he did. Why did he have to lie to me, Mom, and Dad by saying that everything was done and ready? Why did he use the money sent for the house to buy goods for himself, when he knew I was coming back? I didn't know why, and I could not figure out his behaviors. It once again proved that poverty makes everyone look out for themselves. He was so obsessed with money that it was able to corrupt his heart; he was so obsessed with money that it was able to change his character; he was so poor that he was willing to lie and steal from an orphan like myself. It would have been more understandable if this individual didn't have anything or was living below poverty. But by the national standard, this person was far better off economically than the average Burkinabè, which made the situation even harder to understand. As time went on, I learned that material possessions were extremely valued in our society and were the means used to classify people. Consequently, people were willing to do anything (corruption, theft, or committing atrocities) to raise their social class at the expense of another. Sadly, while some struggle to meet their daily necessities, others are obsessed with social class and status.

Once I had learned about everything that had happened with the house, the land, and the money, I called Dad and Mom and told them everything. They too were shocked and surprised. There was nothing they could do, and I didn't know what to do. We were separated by thousands of miles and even if they were in the country, what could they do? I decided to go see Pastor Paul and tell him everything that had happened; I asked him what I should do. The only advice he had for me was to talk to the person who was supposed to get the house built, so I decided to confront him about the situation. Despite many conversations over several weeks, nothing was accomplished with him. It was a waste of my time. I decided to contact the local police department to intervene. I went to the station and explained the whole situation to the police chief. He then assigned another officer to be in charge of the case. However, that officer told me that before he could start the investigation, I needed to pay him money for gas first. He was asking me for ten thousand CFA, which is the equivalent of twenty U.S. dollars. I knew that they did not need my money, and wanted something from me because I had just returned from the United States. I didn't know what to do—take part in bribery and corruption and hopefully get the issue resolved, or leave the police station and be out of everything Dad and Mom had sent for me. I knew that corruption was a big problem in Burkina-Faso and that we needed to do something about it, but here I was now stuck in the middle of it and didn't know how to respond. After deep thinking and weighing the pros and cons, I decided to pay the money to the officer so that he could start the investigation.

During this time, Dad and Mom called a woman they knew and asked her if I could stay with her family until the police department resolved my housing situation. She kindly agreed to their request. In exchange for her hospitality, I helped the family with their daily chores and in whatever other ways I could. Although staying with them was better than being homeless, I felt very uncomfortable there and could never be myself. There was a very strong tension, because I felt like they were constantly waiting for me to make a mistake so that they could report it to Dad and Mom. I am not sure what their motivations were, but it seemed that they wanted me to go back to being a poor lonely orphan. They thought that if I made a mistake and they let Dad and

Mom know about it, that Dad and Mom would stop loving me and sending money to help support me. I sensed that they were against me and were seeking opportunities to make me fall.

For this reason, Dad and Mom thought it would be better for me to find another place to stay. It was then that I decided to rent an apartment that was very close to the YFC school, as school was about to resume. I finally found an apartment about one mile from YFC at the renting price of ten thousand CFA (twenty dollars) per month. It was a one-bedroom apartment with no running water or electricity. I still had to go and buy water at the fountain, but it wasn't far from the apartment. I had a nice battery-operated lamp to use that Dad and Mom had purchased for me while I was in the United States, so the electricity was not a big problem. I was very pleased with the apartment, and it finally put a stable roof over my head. Most apartments in the United States come furnished with a kitchen, refrigerator, stove, bathroom, and closets, but in my apartment there were none of those things. It had just a simple cement floor with no furnishings. However, I did buy some pictures and paintings to decorate with, and also a table and chair so that I would have somewhere to sit. The whole apartment compound had one restroom to share together. It was just a hole in the ground, so it had a terrible smell. Our wash basin— which consisted of a bucket with some water—was in the same room. Although sometimes revolting, most people in Burkina-Faso use these same kinds of facilities. Only the rich people have Westernized bathrooms in their homes.

The apartment complex had four apartments, and all the other apartments were occupied. I was surrounded by neighbors, which helped to make me feel safer than living by myself. After moving my belongings to my new home, I purchased the materials I needed to cook for myself. Cooking was much cheaper and cleaner than eating out all the time. I bought a miniature stove which required kerosene. I did not have a refrigerator to store food or leftovers, which meant that I would only cook the amount of food I needed for that day or the next. I learned to cook rice, beans, pasta, spaghetti, and meat. Though that list would seem short and unimpressive to most Americans, not all Burkinabè could afford these types of food. Most daily diets in Burkina-Faso consist of grains such as sorghum, millet, rice, or maize, peanuts, potatoes, beans, yams and "tô," which is a stiff white porridge made of either white millet or sorghum and served with all kind of sauces. Most foods in Burkina-Faso are eaten with some form of sauce, and meat is a luxury for most people. Tô and other foods like it are eaten everyday because they are relatively inexpensive. Even though the quantity is marginally enough, the quality of the food is not sufficient, and people do not eat a balanced diet. Consequently, most children suffer from malnutrition and inadequate weight problems, from not having the protein and vitamins that their bodies need. It is very common to see children who are twelve or fifteen years old look a lot younger than their ages, due to lack of proper nutrition. Because of the support that Dad and Mom gave me, I was able to have an adequate diet. I was also able to purchase a mattress for myself and for the first time in my life—with the exception of my stay in America—I was not sleeping on the hard floor.

Once I had been settled in my apartment for a few weeks, I had yet to hear back from the police officer in charge of my case, so I decided to go talk to him. When I got to the station, he told me that he was still looking and searching for the right time to go and get the person who was responsible and bring him to justice for his acts. Even though I had paid him "gas" money—which I figured he probably used for food and beer—nothing had been accomplished. Since the police were unable to catch the person, I asked the officer if there was anything I could do to help them. He told me it would be great if I could organize a rendezvous with the person who stole the money. This would then allow the officers to catch him by surprise. After thinking it through, I came up with a plan to catch him. I was going to tell him that Franklin, the American missionary, had phoned and wanted to speak with him. It was an honor to talk to the Americans, so I figured this would be a surefire way to get him to the rendezvous point. I talked to the officers and told them the plan.

Once the situation was all set up, I grew unsettled about what I was doing. I knew that this man had wronged me, but I did not want to send him to jail. His going to jail did not guarantee that the situation would be resolved, as the police were not trustworthy. As these doubts came to my mind, the police arrived. They handcuffed the man and searched him before taking him to jail. Seeing him taken really broke my heart. I wished we were able to resolve the situation between us, without having the police take him. I knew that locking him up wasn't the best option, and what he really needed was a radical change of heart. Only Jesus Christ and a loving heart could change his ways, not the corrupted, messed-up legal system. By this time, I thought I had made a mistake by sending him to jail.

Regardless of how I felt, I still needed to check in at the police station to see if the police were able to resolve the situation. When I got there, I spoke with the officer in charge of my case. He brought the guy into his office; he was in chains and was wearing dirty clothes. I could tell that he had lost some weight and it saddened me. He was not being fed enough while in jail. Worse yet, I could tell he had been abused and beaten—the police had obviously been trying to get information out of him. Prisoners don't have any human rights in Burkina-Faso, and seeing him like that made me sad and bitter about our legal system. I hoped the officer would have good news to share. However, as he told me what he had discovered, things became worse. Apparently, this guy had sold my land to two different people in order to get more money, so he had even more people angry with him. The officer found that this guy owned his own house, so, as a way to pay me back for the wrongdoing, the police wanted me to take his house. Although I was getting the bad end of the deal—the land and money he stole from Dad and Mom was more than what his house was worth—I agreed to it so that the man could be released from jail. Within the next three days, we completed all of the paperwork to transfer his house to me.

I called Dad and Mom and reported everything that happened. We were all glad that the situation was over and the person was released from jail. However, many people came and told me to be very careful with the man who had stolen from me. They told me that he wanted to seek vengeance against me for sending him to jail and for losing his house and they advised me to take extra caution. I didn't know what he wanted to do to me, but I knew he was very angry at me and would surely attempt to get revenge. At that point, I didn't know what to do, or where to go and hide. I just kept my eyes opened while praying for God to protect me from those who wanted to harm me. Because of these safety issues, Mom, Dad and I decided to sell the house right away. I could return to my apartment and live there—having the neighbors added extra security. Without any delay, I started to market the house for sale and surprisingly, within a week, the house was sold at a price of two hundred thousand CFA, which is the equivalent to four hundred U.S. dollars.

I was happy to have the whole issue resolved. I did not harbor any bad feelings toward this man who had stolen from me, but I was tired of dealing with the situation and gladly moved on. Once I got settled again in the apartment, I decided to go back to Sandéba to visit François and Idrissa. On my way to the village, I bought two bags of rice to give to François to help him take care of his family, and bought some bread for the children. Most families did not have access to bread, so the children thought it was a treat. I also gave François some money to help him with school fees. Everyone gave me a very warm welcome, although I am not sure if they were really excited to see me or if they were just happy that I brought gifts. François was very happy that

I did not forget about him. In typical fashion, he made me feel guilty about not writing him while I was in America, although I told him that I had no way of contacting him. He was very curious about America and asked me many questions about what it looked like, what the people were like, and how Americans farmed. While I was visiting with them, I thought so much about the grace and the blessings of God in my life. I was very thankful to the Lord for raising me up above the abuse, persecution, and abandonment that I had suffered as a child. My family had thought I was a nobody, but the Lord blessed me in more ways than I ever thought possible. He had not blessed me because of anything I had done, but because he loved me so much. Tears came down from my eyes—I could not help but cry when I thought about God's grace, his blessings and everything he has done for me. He is indeed the father of the fatherless and he anointed my head with oil.

After visiting with François and the other people in the village, I returned to the city and my apartment. Even though I was living alone, I still talked to Dad and Mom on a regular basis. I continued to remain in contact with them through phone calls and letters. They agreed to call me every two weeks, and while I was settling into my new apartment, Dad and Mom bought me a new bicycle. This made it so much easier to get to school and other places; it was like a dream come true. I enjoyed it very much and kept it clean every day. Once I purchased the bicycle I went and showed it to Francis, Pastor Paul, Pastor Jean, and others. I also took a picture of the bike and sent it to Dad and Mom so they too could see what it was like.

I also was able to get my own mailbox at the post office, so that I was able to receive my own mail instead of having it go through another source before it got to me. This way I no longer had to worry about people opening up my letters and stealing money from me. Once I got the mailbox, I wrote to most of my friends in the United States and gave them my address. Now that I had my own mailbox, everything was in place for us to keep in touch and I was sure I would get their letters if they wrote to me. In addition to getting the mailbox, Dad and Mom advised me to open a savings account at the bank instead of keeping so much cash on me. I was glad to have my own account and not have to worry about thieves breaking into my apartment and stealing my money. Once the savings account was opened, I learned how to manage my money better and I even learned how to balance my savings book. It also helped that I had access to a Western Union. Dad and Mom were able to send money quickly, and I didn't have to wait three or four weeks to get it through the mail—I could then buy the things I needed and save the rest of the money. Even though I did not have a lot of money at the bank, I felt like I was among the elite. Many people in Burkina-Faso do not have money to meet their daily needs, let alone money to save; the majority of the population does not have any reason to step in a bank. Mostly those people with disposable incomes visited the bank. Every time I went there to make a deposit, I was surprised at the amount of money that was exchanged there. The wealthy customers would come in either to deposit or withdraw thousands of CFAs, holding more money in their hands at one time than I had ever seen before.

This world of the elite rich was very new to me. Although I didn't have nearly as much money as they, I was able to witness how flippant some of them were about money. I wondered how they could be like that when many of their countrymen were dying of starvation. Why was it that some could afford huge houses and air-conditioned cars when others had to walk everywhere and had to live in buildings that were barely habitable? The children of the rich went to study at European or American schools, while the rest of the country remained uneducated. The gap between the rich and the poor is very great in Third World countries, much more so than in modern nations. I was saddened and angered by the social injustice I saw. Most of the wealthy people were merchants or government workers or doctors—all of whom earned one paycheck from their jobs and another from bribery and corruption. They were taking money from those who had next to nothing, and those whose children were starving, just so that they could have bigger homes and better cars. I could almost taste the bitterness I felt.

Again my mind questioned how this kind of evil could exist, and where God was in the midst of all the misery. I began to pray the prayers of the prophet Habakkuk when he, too, witnessed injustice: "Why do you make me look at injustice? Why do you tolerate wrong? Destruction and violence are before me. There is strife, and conflict abounds. Therefore the law is paralyzed, and justice never prevails. The wicked hem in the righteous, so that justice is perverted" (Habakkuk 1:3-4). These thoughts and questions were always on my mind, even when I went about my business during a normal day.

-9-
A NEW LIFE IN AFRICA

All hard work brings a profit, but mere talk leads to poverty.
>   —Proverbs 14:2

On September 15 of that year, we began school again. Because I had left the previous year a month early to go to America, the school officials told me that if I wanted to stay at YFC, I had to repeat 11th grade. If I did not want to do that, I was told I would have to change schools. I chose the easier option and repeated the 11th grade. I was excited for school to start. Now that I had a secure home, food to eat, a bicycle to get around, and a little money in the bank, I had nothing left that would distract me from my studies. In addition, I had enough spare time that I could get a job.

Even though Dad and Mom were supporting me financially, I knew that I needed to do something to help myself instead of depending on them all the time. In Africa, we have a proverb: "If someone is washing your back, you need to wash the front of your body yourself." Although I truly appreciated their help, I did not like the feeling of being totally dependent. Sometimes I told them I had enough money when I really didn't. Many times when I needed something they were more than willing to get for me, I said I didn't need it. It felt like I was begging them for the things I needed, and I hated that. I wanted to earn my own living instead of having someone give me what I needed. I was never okay with them sending me money time after time, but I was always grateful for their generosity and compassion toward me, and I learned to accept their help.

In the midst of looking for a part-time job, I was offered a position at YFC to dust, sweep and mop the administration building once a day, which I usually completed after work and school hours. It wasn't really a hard job—just a little bit time consuming. I only earned five thousand CFA (ten dollars) a month. Even though I wasn't making much, it was enough to help me buy food and water for drinking, cooking, and laundry because I didn't have running water at my apartment. Some of my friends were surprised that I was doing that kind of work because I had just returned from America, and they thought I either already had money, or that I would be doing more respectable jobs. They wondered why I was doing the so-called "dirty work" that they themselves wouldn't do. It is an interesting dichotomy; most Burkinabè, no matter how poor, are not willing to do what is considered "dirty work." Many people from other African nations such as Ghana will do just about any work in order to make a living, whether this means selling water, washing clothes, doing domestic work, selling merchandise, or collecting trash. Burkinabè, on the other hand, are not willing to do those jobs. They view them as demeaning jobs, and so they would rather not work at all than do them. They would rather gather with other people under trees to drink their tea or coffee and listen to their music. To most Burkinabè, it is more respectable not to have any job than to do the nonrespectable ones.

I was able to handle working on top of my school work with no problems. Out of all the subjects I was taking, the subject that I had improved the most in over the summer break was English. Of course, going to the United States helped improve my English tremendously, as did writing letters to Dad and Mom and my other friends in the States. Even though it was still not at the level of a native speaker, I was far ahead of the other students in my class. I didn't need to put a lot of effort into that subject. However, even though English came easily to me, I still did my best and submitted my homework. Some of my friends would come to me and ask me for help with their homework and class projects in the English subject. I became a tutor again, like I once had been in the village.

Ever since I started school I have had the desire to succeed and be at the top, and I was determined that neither past nor present circumstances would prevent that from happening. Now more than ever I had the motivation and determination to succeed—I wanted to show Dad and Mom that I could be the best. I had always achieved high grades, even when I was poor and starving; now at least I could concentrate on my work and not on my growling belly. Surprisingly, some of the rich children, even though they had everything they needed, did not do well in school. They were spoiled with so many toys that they did not have time to study. They didn't have the will, the desire and the motivation to succeed academically. I had people supporting me and I felt very grateful to be able to attend school, which is why I wanted to do my best and not take it for granted. I worked really hard that year, and as a result, I was among the top students in the whole school. I was very anxious to report my grades to Dad, Mom, Pastor Paul, and others. They were all pleased with my performance, and they all congratulated me. Through school, I could prove to Dad and Mom that I was not the person that everyone tried to tell them I was before leaving for America. They were proud of me and my hard work.

Despite my happiness about doing well in school, there was one thing that still hung over my head like a dark cloud. The person who had stolen the land from me and had gone to jail found out where my apartment was. Several people warned me that he still wanted to seek revenge. I had no idea what he planned to do or what he was capable of, and fear dominated my mind. It was especially bad at night. I would always lock myself in my apartment, because the majority of bad things happened during the night. Many times I had nightmares about him coming after me and trying to harm me. I wished I had a roommate so that I would feel safer. I couldn't wait for morning to come because of how much fear I had at night. Several times during the night I heard someone knocking on my door, and I didn't know if it was him. I didn't even dare cough or open the door to see who it was, because I was scared. To feel a little more secure, I made sure that I had two locks on my door. My fear seemed to be unbearable at times, and I knew that there was only one person who could take it away—Jesus Christ. As I had done many times before, I decided several times to go and see Pastor Jean and asked him to pray for me so that God would protect me from danger.

In the spring of 1999, Dad and Mom informed me that they were going to be coming to Burkina-Faso on another medical mission trip to be headed by Franklin Spotts. I was very happy that I would get to see them again. In my heart, I think they had two reasons to come back to Burkina-Faso. The first, and probably the greater reason, was because they wanted to see me, and the second reason was to help other people. I couldn't wait for them to see my apartment, where I was living, and my new bike. Ever since I had returned from the United States, I missed them very much. I was so anxious to see them that I started counting down the days until their arrival. The time couldn't go fast enough.

On Sunday, March 7, 1999, Dad and Mom once again landed in Burkina-Faso, along with five other Americans. I went to the airport to welcome them, and as soon as I saw them coming out of the gate, I ran and hugged them and wouldn't let them go. We were all smiling. It was so good to see them again and be with them. I met the three other Americans who were a part of the team. Once we had all greeted each other, we all went to Wend and Celestine's house. After they unpacked and were all settled, I started asking about everybody that I knew in the United States. Dad and Mom brought me some goodies: a pair of shoes, a couple of shirts and pants, and surprisingly, two cans of Mountain Dew. Wow! I couldn't believe it. I poured it into a glass and let the others taste it. They all liked it and wanted more and more.

Shortly before they all went to bed, Pastor Paul came to discuss with the missionaries the plans for their time in Burkina-Faso. The team was going to be in Burkina-Faso for two weeks, and then in Mali (a country located northwest of Burkina-Faso) for ten days. During their time in each of these countries, they would treat people who were suffering from all kinds of diseases. After Pastor Paul was done talking, he gave them all time to get settled in and rested up for the next day.

When it came time for bed, I didn't want to go back and sleep at my apartment. I wanted to stay with Dad and Mom and everybody else at the house. I had a hard time preparing to leave them, then I saw that Mom had already prepared a place for me to sleep in the living room. I was very happy that I did not have to leave them. I went back to my apartment, packed a bag full of clothes, gathered my school materials, and took everything back to the house. It was a good feeling to be with Dad and Mom again and I wished that they were going to stay forever.

The next morning, I got up before everyone else and started to get ready for school. As soon as I saw that Dad and Mom were awake, I took them outside the house and showed them my bicycle. They were very pleased finally to see it for themselves. Dad even got on it and acted as if he was going to take it for a ride, but instead they took pictures of it. It was interesting to me how Dad and Mom loved taking pictures of everything they saw.

After I showed Dad and Mom my bicycle and left for school, the team started going to their locations to treat people. There is always a need for people who can help with medical conditions in Burkina-Faso, and these missionaries were back for the third year in a row. As expected, hundreds, if not thousands, of people came from all over to be treated by the Americans. Many had diseases that I had never heard of, while others had infections on their bodies that looked and smelled awful. Even though most of the missionaries on the team did not have medical degrees, they had a basic knowledge of how to treat sicknesses, which is something that many Burkinabè do not have.

In the evening after they had returned from treating people and were well rested, Dad, Mom and I, along with other people, decided to go see my apartment. I opened the door and entered into the apartment and showed them what it was like inside. They told me they liked it and that it was a nice place; they took pictures of it as well. As soon as the children in the neighborhood saw Dad and Mom with me, they came and surrounded them as if they had never seen white people. Some were begging for money, others wanted to hold their hands, while others were fighting just to be able to touch them. Some of the adults even came from their houses to see them. They wouldn't stop staring at them. I was very embarrassed by their behavior and I wanted to tell them to go away. I felt that such behaviors were degrading the dignity and self-worth of the entire black race because they were placing people on a pedestal because of their skin color and nationality.

After Dad and Mom had been in Burkina-Faso for a week, they told me that they were planning to bring me back to the United States during the summer holiday. Considering the cost of an airplane ticket, I was overwhelmed. There were no words to say. I was more than happy, and was looking forward for school to end so that I could leave for the United States. Before they left the country, all three of us went to the United States Embassy to talk to them about granting me a visa. We did not apply for the visa at that time, but we only went to see if it was going to be possible for me to get another one, and to see if there were going to be any questions that Dad and Mom should answer while they were still in the country. The consular we talked to told us that it would be no problem for me to get a visa since I had returned to the country from my previous trip.

When the day came for the missionaries to leave for Mali, it was very sad to see them leave, and it was even harder to say goodbye to Dad and Mom. They had touched the lives of so many people. I remember crying as they were packing and getting ready to go to the airport and then standing at the airport and watching their plane take off until I could not see it anymore. Despite how hard it was to see them leave, I had peace in my heart for I knew that I was going to see them again very soon. I could hardly wait for school to end so that I could be with them again.

I went back to my apartment that night and cried because I was so overwhelmed with the thought of how God was turning my life around. He had blessed me beyond what I could ever have dreamt, and I was grateful for all that he was doing.

10

RETURNING TO MY "NEW HOME"

They overcame him by the blood of the Lamb and by the word of their testimony.
—Revelation 12:11

Because I had just been to the United States the previous summer, some of the documents I needed in order to travel had not yet expired. Thankfully, I did not have to do as much work as the first time I had gone to America. My passport and health requirements were still valid for me to travel, so all I needed was my visa to the United States and the airplane ticket that Dad and Mom had already purchased for me. I did not need a letter from François this time because I was eighteen, which made the process much easier. Before I started applying for my visa to the United States, I fasted and prayed, asking for God's favor once again. I even went to see Pastor Jean and together we prayed and pleaded for God's grace and favor to be upon me.

After we had prayed and fasted, I went to the United States embassy and got an application for the visa. I had established trust with the U.S. Embassy because I had kept my word and had returned to the country after my first trip. Usually people leave the country and never return. Some of the people who were working at the embassy remembered me, which was an advantage for me. I applied for the visa, paid the visa fees (fifty thousand CFA or one hundred dollars), and went and deposited it at the embassy. I then had an interview with the consular. Before the interview, Dad and Mom had sent a letter by fax from the United States, pleading on my behalf that the consular grant me my visa to the United States. On the day of the interview, the consular asked me several questions and then told me to come back at four o'clock in the afternoon. I was so nervous that I couldn't sit still or eat or do anything at all. All I had on my mind was four o'clock. I kept praying. When the time finally arrived and I was at the embassy, I took a seat among many other people who were waiting for their visas. The consular began calling names and handing out passports to people. She soon called my name, and I got up and went and got my passport and told the lady, "Thank you."

I had my visa to the United States once again! I was overwhelmed with joy and I hurried and called Dad and Mom to tell them I had my visa. They too were very happy and excited for me. I also went and showed it to Pastor Jean and together we thanked God for granting me the visa. I now had all the different documents that I needed to travel to the United States. Unlike my first trip, when I saw so much opposition to my going to America, this time there was no opposition at all. There was complete and total silence even from those who had sought to oppose my trip the year before. Along with Pastor Jean, I thanked the Lord for silencing our enemies and shutting down their lying lips.

Before I left the country, I made sure that I put all my

belongings into my apartment and locked them up because of all the things that had happened last time I was gone. I told my neighbor and the landlord that I was traveling to the United States, and I asked them to keep an eye on my apartment. I paid the landlord for three months of rent before leaving, because I knew I would be gone for the months of June, July, and August. Even though I did not want my stuff stolen, I wasn't really concerned about it; all I cared about was that I was going back to the United States. I went and said my good-byes to my friends, and I even went to the village to say good-bye to François and everybody else that I knew.

After two days of traveling, I finally landed in the United States. I was happy to be back, and even more overjoyed to see and be with Dad and Mom again. I had missed them so much while in Burkina-Faso. Within a few days of arrival, I was able to see my American brothers and sisters, my friends, and everyone else that I knew. I even went to see Dr. Ellis and Dr. Cummins to show them my leg. It was completely healed, but the scars were still there for them to see. They were very happy that the infection was gone. I thanked them very much for everything that they had done for me. I took the time to thank God Almighty for bringing me back, and to thank him for everything he was doing in my life. He has surely blessed me so much and I thought the least I could do in return was to say, "Thank You."

Once I was settled, I started helping Dad do some plumbing, electrical, and construction work at my brother's race track. I remember seeing them use heavy, high-tech machines at the construction sites—this was something I had rarely seen in Burkina-Faso. I remember the good times Dad and I had together while working—the times for lunches when we would run to the nearby restaurants, the stories he shared with me, the laughter and joy I experienced while working with him. I also remember how frustrating it was when we had to redo everything because something went wrong or we left something out. I remember Dad teaching me how to drive his truck. That was the first time I had been behind the wheel; what a joy that was for me. Most importantly, by working with Dad, I also came to know who he is as a person—his great personality, his strong Christian faith and his incorruptible character. I also saw his compassion and caring for those who are less fortunate.

On June 15, Dad, Mom, and I went to Waynesfield Methodist Church for a lunch to help the youth raise money for Lakeside church camp. The youth asked me if I wanted to go to camp with them. I hesitated at first, not knowing whether to go or not. The camp was to last for one week and I wasn't sure if I wanted to leave Dad and Mom for that long. Two of their grandchildren, Chandra and Colby Shobe, as well as other people that I knew, were going. There were twenty-three youth from the United Methodist church in Waynesfield, and several adults as the team leaders, who were also going to camp. The registration cost was two hundred dollars, and I didn't want Dad and Mom to spend that much money on me. They insisted that I not worry about the money. Since Chandra and Colby were going, and since there were other people that I know from Waynesfield going, I decided to go as well. It would be my first time to attend a church camp, so I didn't really know what it was or everything that it involved. Even when we were on our way to the church camp, I remember telling one of the team leaders that I wanted to return home instead of going. However, they did not take me back home, and eventually I was excited to go.

I didn't know how many would be attending the camp, but when I got there, I realized that it was a huge crowd of young people who came from all over Ohio. I don't know the exact number of people who were there, but there were at least three hundred young people accompanied by adult team leaders. At first, I didn't know how to respond to it. I don't like being in a huge crowd of people, but since there were people I knew, I was okay. There was a whole house specifically for the youth from Waynesfield. It was a two-story house. The adults who were with us decided to put the boys on the first floor and the girls on the second floor.

Once settled, we were ready to start the different activities that were planned. The camp leaders gave us a bulletin which contained the dates, times, locations, and speakers for the different events. They had different speakers from all over the United States to speak on various biblical topics. A normal day would consist of morning prayer, teaching, Bible study, lunch, and then free time. During the free time, people usually went shopping in the nearby stores or played sports such as tennis or basketball. Lakeside was surrounded by a beautiful lake, and during free time, people would walk around or sit by the edge of the lake to relax their minds, watch the birds, or pray. I personally enjoyed being at the lake, watching the birds fly back and forth and watching the waves of the water. The afternoon would usually consist of teachings, dinner, and Bible study. Before going to bed, our team leaders usually got all the youth from our group to have our own Bible study and prayer time. During those times, people usually shared about things they were dealing with and then we would pray for each other's prayer requests.

During that week, we heard one speaker after another, men and women of God, preaching and teaching us the word of God. Some had a Pentecostal approach, others combined humor with the word of God to make a fun show, still others were very simple and direct. Despite their different styles of preaching, we saw many people come to the altar and accept Jesus Christ as their Lord and Savior, and that was what mattered most. On many occasions during that week, I was overwhelmed with joy and thanksgiving when I saw youth crying and weeping as they ran to the altar and gave their lives to Jesus of Nazareth. Their friends were there to cry and celebrate with them as they were about to begin a new life with Jesus Christ. I wondered what heaven was like. I am sure the angels were overwhelmed with joy and were singing and praising God for the decisions of those young people.

While at camp, I got to meet other people and made a lot of friends. I developed good relationships with our team leaders. One day, as we were having our Bible study before bed time, I shared a little bit about my life and what I had encountered while I was in Africa. The youth and the team leaders were surprised at what I had gone through as a young boy in Africa. They contacted the camp leaders and asked them if they could allow me to share my testimony with everybody else at camp. At first, I had mixed feelings about it. I told them that I would pray and think about it to see if I should do it. The more I prayed and thought, the more I didn't want to do it. I didn't want to re-live the past. However, I felt that God was telling me to share my testimony, not only to show what he has done for me, but also what he could do for other people in their lives—regardless of what they were going through. I told the team leaders that I would do it. However, I told them that in order for me to express myself effectively, it would be very helpful if they could find someone to translate from French to English. The camp leaders made an announcement to the whole crowd, trying to find someone who spoke French. But no one came forward.

The same day, it happened that one girl's mom came to pick her up because she had to leave early. It happened that she was a French teacher, so they asked her if she could stay and translate for me the next day. She agreed to the request. Together with her, my team leader, and others, I sat down and told them my testimony with a message at the end. They typed out the overview and everything that I was going to say the next day. After we were done, I went back with the youth to the house. We prayed together for the next day, and for God to be with me as I was going to speak to the people.

The next day, around ten in the morning, they put me on stage, along with Lynn Davis. I began to share the pieces of my testimony that we had written the night before. I shared in French, and Lynn translated into English. Even though it wasn't the first time I had been in front of a crowd of people, towards the end I became very emotional. I got upset about the things that had happened to me, and was re-living the past. I began crying and weeping and then left and went back to the house where we were staying. I remember being sad for most of that day and not even eating. I refused to participate in events for the rest of that day. I just wanted to be alone in my bedroom. Yet I was surprised by the love and support I received from the youth and team leaders from Waynesfield. The team leaders and the other youth came over and tried to hug me and console me. I don't know if they knew what I was going through, but they did know how to sympathize with my feelings. For the remainder of the time that we were at camp, everywhere I went, people wanted a copy of my testimony. They wanted to talk to me about what I had gone through, and they all wanted my address. I made many friends. My testimony was the highlight of the week—even though it was not the main event.

After I returned from church camp, Dad, Mom, and I went to the Harrod Pork Rind festival. Surprisingly, I ran across LeeAnn Shade—one of the women who had helped translate my testimony at church camp. We exchanged phone numbers and addresses, and she talked to me about coming to speak at Teens for Christ (TFC), which is a group of youth who get together to study the word of God and spread the gospel to other youth in communities around the world. I went and spoke at TFC, and soon after that LeeAnn arranged with several churches to have me share my testimony with the congregation before leaving for Africa. I spent most of my remaining time in the United States speaking at TFC and the local churches in Ohio. More than sharing the specifics of my testimony, I shared the reality of those in Africa who are suffering. I was no longer excited about sharing my testimony, but more excited to inspire and challenge the Christians in America to think deeply about their role as Christians in the midst of suffering in the world.

Dad, Mom, and LeeAnn started looking for colleges for me to attend the next year, after I graduated from high school. They called colleges and universities in Michigan, Ohio, Indiana, and Kentucky. They were trying to find a school that would give good scholarships to international students. I was so excited to see that this could actually be a reality for me. I was behind the scenes, praying for God to bring along a good Christian school and to work out all the details and finances. In the midst of looking for a school, a neighbor to Dad and Mom who was attending Bluffton College (now Bluffton University), asked me if I wanted to go to school with her to meet one of her professors who was from Africa. He was from Cameroon, a country in the central part of Africa. After class was over, I got a chance to talk with Dr. Asuabor and explained to him that I was looking for a school to attend the following year. He promised me that he would look into it and see how he could help. I was happy that night not only for meeting another brother from Africa, but also for the possibility that he could help me get admitted to the school. I made sure that we exchanged addresses before I left the country.

By the second week in August, the time for me to return to Africa was getting closer and closer. This time, Dad and Mom had something that they were secretly planning before my return. They revealed their plans to me as the date grew closer; because I was not going to be here on my birthday, they were going to throw me a birthday party in advance. I didn't realize how huge the party was going to be until the day arrived. They rented a tent and invited a lot of family and friends from the church, as well as many people I had met at Lakeside church camp earlier that summer. I didn't really know how to respond at first. After all, I didn't really know my real birth date, and this was the first time ever that I or anybody else had ever celebrated my birthday—even my own mom had never done such a thing. In Burkina-Faso, it is very uncommon to celebrate one's birthday. It is just not a big deal to anyone other than the rich—who have the resources to plan such celebrations.

Soon after church was dismissed on August 8, we began preparing a lot of food for the party. At five o'clock in the afternoon, the people started coming. I was overwhelmed by the number of cars and people that came. Some people even came from far distances to celebrate at the party with us. Boy, what a party it was! We ate, we talked, and we shared fellowship with one another. Many of the people who came brought me presents. Regardless of what they brought, it touched my heart that people had come from near and far just for me. After the party was over, late that evening, I was grateful that Dad and Mom would do so much work just for me. I thanked God for that day. It was good to see everyone, especially those I had met during Lakeside church camp. Towards the end of the party, it was hard saying good-bye to the people I met because I wasn't going to see them for a while. I was getting ready to go back to Africa. Everyone was lining up to say good-bye, hugging me, telling me that they loved me and that they were going to miss me, and exchanging addresses. I was overwhelmed that I had so many friends who loved me and cared about me.

As I was getting ready to return to Burkina-Faso, the youth I had met at Teens For Christ collected money and bought a very nice guitar for me. All the youth signed their names on the belt. I was really surprised by their generosity; I wished I knew how to play it. I thanked them for the guitar and soon, LeeAnn began teaching me how to play the guitar as well as to read music. Surprisingly, by the time I was to return to Burkina-Faso, I knew how to play specific songs and even make a melody.

Unlike the first time, when it was so hard to leave, this time it was much easier because I knew I had a great chance of returning for college the following year. It was still hard to leave Dad and Mom and the United States and go back to Africa. I remember crying many times, not wanting to think or talk about going back home. By then, even though Burkina-Faso was my country, I surely had another home in the United States. I also had a family, which made it harder to leave and return to an empty home in Africa. There, I didn't have anyone who truly cared about and loved me. Here, I had parents, brothers and sisters and friends who truly cared about and loved me. I remember crying and weeping aloud from the time we left home until we arrived at the airport. I remember holding Mom's hands tightly, telling her over and over that I love her and not to forget me. Once at the airport, when it was time for me to get in the plane, I remember holding Dad and Mom and not wanting to let go of them until they were about to close the gate. We hugged over and over, crying and weeping and not wanting to part from each other. I spent more of that day crying than smiling.

11

EYES FIXED ON THE GOAL

Therefore, since we are surrounded by such a great cloud of witnessing, let us throw off everything that hinders and the sin that so easily entangles, and let us run with perseverance the race marked for us. Let us fix our eyes on Jesus, the author and perfecter of our faith....
—Hebrews 12:1-2

Soon after I returned home from the United States and was settled back into my apartment, I was ready to tackle my final year of high school. The opportunity to go to an American college was looking very promising. However, in order to graduate, like everybody else, I had to pass the national exam. If I did not pass that exam, I would have to repeat the same grade again. The stakes were high for me, so my focus was on school and nothing else. Many people quit school because they get tired of taking it over and over. I wasn't concerned about getting a job or doing activities—my one goal was to pass the exam.

The exam was to take place in June, and no one knew what the exam was going to look like. We just tried to study hard. That year, from September to June, I did nothing but study and pray for God's help. I was sleeping less and less because I was constantly studying. A couple of us even formed a group to study together and help one another with questions. For me, failure was not an option. My goal was to pass the exam on the first try, and not delay the possibility of going to the United States to study. The Lord had always blessed me with knowledge in school, and I had always done well. He had always made me the head, and not the tail, and I believed in my heart that I was going to pass the exam and the following year be on my way to the United States.

In April of 2000, of the different universities that we checked out, Bluffton College was showing some interest in me. They sent the application, which I filled out and sent back to them. They requested that I write an essay about why I wanted to attend their school, along with my goals and vision; they also wanted a copy of my transcript. Soon after they received my application, they set up a specific date and time to call me on the phone to have an interview to test my understanding, comprehension, and proficiency in English. When it came time for the call, I talked to Dr. Eric Fullcomer, who was the director of admissions for Bluffton College at the time. I worried about whether or not Dr. Fullcomer thought my English was good enough and whether or not I was going to be admitted. I prayed and left the matter up to God, for I knew that if he said "yes," then no one in the heavens, on the earth, or beneath the earth, could say "no."

At that point, I was optimistic that I would be heading to the United States as long as I passed my exam. I had a lot of pressure to succeed. I asked Dad and Mom if they could help me afford a private tutor in mathematics for part of April and May, and they agreed to help me. Math was five credit hours and if you could get a good grade in that subject, along with at least a "C" for the rest of the subjects, you could surely pass the exam. It wasn't my favorite subject, and knowing the importance of it, I wanted to be good at it. My own math teacher agreed to be my private tutor outside of school. After school, I would meet with him for four hours each week, and we would go over homework, exercises, and anything that I didn't understand. In return, I paid him one thousand three hundred CFA, or three dollars, per hour. With his help, my confidence level was high, and by the end of May, I was as prepared as I could be for the exam.

As the exam date drew closer, many were going to witch doctors for magic help, and the rich children were trying to buy the exam before the set date. I went to God and asked him to be with me, and to bless me with knowledge as I took the exam. Some people knew that I was going to the States to study if I passed my exam, and their prayers were that I would fail the exam, so that I would have to stay in Burkina-Faso. For that reason, I pleaded with God day and night, asking him not to allow my "enemies" to triumph over me, but once again to give me victory over them. God surely heard our prayers from heaven, and I had faith he would answer them as he promised in Matthew 7:7: "Ask and it will be given to you."

On June 5, I got to my place bright and early in the morning before the exam started. I couldn't afford to be late, because if you are late you automatically fail the exam—unless you have a serious illness. There were many people there when I arrived at the school, all nervously waiting to start the exam. Around 7:30 a.m., they began calling our names and placing us into the exam rooms. There were at least three people in every room to supervise and make sure that people were not cheating. The first day, we had French and English on the exam. I felt pretty good about the English at the end. I thought it was easy. On the second day, we had biology, history, and geography. On the third day, we had physics, chemistry, and mathematics. We finished on the fourth day with exercise physiology. I felt pretty good about the exam overall. After we finished taking the exam, we had to wait for three days for the teachers to correct them before revealing the results on the fourth day.

Four days seemed like weeks when the results would determine so much of my life. Everyone was very anxious and couldn't wait for the day that we would know if we had passed or not. I remained on my knees during that period, praying that my exam would fall into the hands of one who would treat me with fairness. There were rumors that some of the teachers weren't reading the exams before correcting them and that some were too drunk even to see the papers at all. There were also rumors that the rich parents were corrupting the teachers with money so that their children would pass. All these reasons made me stay on my knees praying for God to be on my side.

On the day of the results, everyone was there—parents, loved ones, and of course the students themselves. Upon our arrival, the principal began to release the results by reading the names of those who had passed the exam, in alphabetical order. If you didn't hear your name, you had failed and would have to retake the exam the following year. Everyone was nervous and dead silent. Nobody was moving, and we were all praying to hear our names read by the principal. My heart was full of fear and beating so hard. My future was on the line, and it all depended on whether or not I would hear my name.

As the principal reached the T's, I suddenly heard my name. I jumped and ran several laps around the building. I didn't know what to do with myself. I was more than happy. They handed me my diploma that showed that I had passed the exam and officially graduated. As soon as I received the diploma, I left the building and was on my way to go make a phone call to Dad and Mom to inform them that I had passed the exam. I called and screamed on the phone and told them, and they too were very happy. I then went back to my apartment and bought chicken and Fanta, Sprite, and Coca-Cola to celebrate with my neighbors and some of my friends. I also called Pastor Jean, Pastor Paul, and François and told them. They were so happy to hear it. Pastor Jean and I got together and praised God for helping me. I fasted the next day and called it a day of thanksgiving to God for helping me. It was such a wonderful and glorious day, a day that I will never forget. I received several congratulations from friends, teachers, and school officials.

In July of that year, I received my acceptance letter from Bluffton College. Furthermore, I was granted a scholarship of fifty percent of the tuition. The dream was becoming reality, and I could not believe it. I was heading to the United States once again—but this time it wasn't for only three or four months, but up to five years. Once I was accepted, the preparation for going to the United States began.

From July to August, we were able to get the different documents we needed for the visa. I had all the papers showing that I had been accepted to Bluffton College, and that Dad and Mom were responsible for funding my education, so getting my visa was a guarantee. Since I had already been in the United States and returned to Burkina-Faso, the embassy personnel knew and trusted us.

On July 31, 2000, I went for the visa. As expected, I got an F-1 (student visa) for the Unites States. I was on my way to the United States for higher education. What a dream come true!

-12-
HIGHER EDUCATION IN AMERICA

Make a career of humanity...and you will make a greater person of yourself, a greater nation of your country, and a finer world to live in.
　　　　　　　　　　　— Martin Luther King, Jr.

Upon my arrival in the United States, I stayed with Dad and Mom for a couple of weeks before going to school. Even though they took me to the campus to meet the faculty and get familiar with my surroundings before classes started, I was still very nervous about attending. Dad and Mom's house felt familiar to me—it was home—but now I had to move into a strange building with people I had never met who were from a completely different culture than my own. I briefly considered asking Dad and Mom if I could commute for the first semester, but I knew that making a daily drive to and from Bluffton (approximately thirty miles) would have been very inconvenient for them. Although my anxiety was high, so was my excitement. Looking back through my life, I thought it was pretty amazing that an impoverished, starving orphan from a small African country would have the chance to study in the United States!

I thought that getting involved in a campus activity would help me to meet people, feel more comfortable, and perhaps ease my fears. I decided to play soccer because I had grown up playing the game. It is a major sport in Burkina-Faso and all around Africa. But the game I was used to—a few children kicking a makeshift ball around on a dirt field—was a different experience than playing on beautiful grass fields with top-quality equipment. I was surprised at how many students at Bluffton played soccer, considering the fact that soccer is not well-known for being played in the U.S. I met a lot of people and being part of the team helped me feel more at ease about being there. We did a lot of running and weightlifting, and spent a lot of time studying videos of the game. I was more than ready for school to start, because that meant we would not have to do so much conditioning!

The weekend before classes started, all the students moved into the dorms. I had been staying in a temporary room during soccer conditioning, and I finally was able to move to my permanent room and meet my roommate. The experience of moving into a living space with someone you have never met before is unnerving. Of course, many people go to college and become best friends with their roommates. Unfortunately for me, the only thing my roommate and I had in common was the fact that we were both freshmen. He was an African-American student, so at first I was very excited to meet him. I thought that we would understand each other, but that we could also learn a lot from one another. While I was in college to study hard and to learn as much as I could, my roommate seemed to be more interested in going to parties. He liked to play his hip-hop music very loudly, which made it hard to study. He would often invite many people to our room to hang out while listening to loud music. I spent more time in the library or computer lab than in my room because these were the only places I could concentrate. We struggled to get along throughout the semester, and for that reason I felt we would both be better off if we did not continue to share a room. I requested to be moved into a different room and was granted a transfer in the second semester.

Every college student likes to have fun, but I was surprised at how many students were more interested in partying than in studying. Many of them regularly skipped classes because they were too tired from being up late at parties. I knew Dad and Mom had worked hard for the money to pay my tuition, and I felt very blessed to be at college. There was no way I could make having fun more important than getting an education. Many of the American students seemed to take college for granted, though I suppose that would be natural since they had such easy access to it. But for someone from the Third World, even getting through primary school was a big deal. American universities would normally be infinitely out of reach for a person of my background. I wanted so badly to do my best, and therefore I spent a lot of time studying. There was a center on campus that helped students with writing assignments. Since I still struggled with English, I spent a lot of time there. I think maybe I was there too much, and the poor tutors there probably hoped I would just leave them alone! Instead of waiting for the last minute to get my assignments done like most students did, one of my strategies was to get my assignments done a couple of days in advance. I would turn in the rough draft and get feedback from my professors, and then rework it again and again until I was satisfied with it. I was dedicated to earning good grades, despite English being a challenge to me.

During my first semester, I met with the registrar to select a major. I told her that I did not know what I wanted to major in, and she asked me to think about what I wanted to do. I am not sure she understood how deep that question was for me. What did I want to do? I had absolutely no idea, and I did not really even know where to begin. I had been so focused on getting into college and getting off to a good start that I did not stop to look ahead to the future. This question consumed me during my first year of college. I initially chose computer science because that is the field that most of my friends back in Burkina-Faso were going into after high school. However, shortly after I started my first CS course, I knew that it was not for me. I wanted to quit that class halfway through the semester, but I managed to stick it out to the end. I was certain that would be both my first and last computer science course.

As the semester wore on, I still could not figure out what I wanted to do. I thought perhaps youth ministry or maybe pre-med, but I knew that I wanted to work with adults more than youth and that I had no real desire to work in a hospital. Because I could not resolve this issue, I decided to meet with Dr. Asuabor to explain the dilemma I was facing. I was hoping he would have answers for me, but instead he just asked me more questions. Though they were simple questions—"What do you enjoy doing?" "What do you want to do?"—they were impossible for me to answer. Perhaps it was hard for me to think concretely about the future because for most of my life I really had no future to speak of. Of course, as a child I had dreams, but children quickly learn that the reality of life in Africa dashes hopes and thoughts of good things to come. My future now held promise, but my mind could not make that transition so quickly. To be able actually to choose my life path was a very new experience for me. I left Dr. Asuabor's office feeling frustrated at my inability to answer his questions. For the rest of the day, those questions weighed on my mind. I was focused on finding the answers, and I prayed that God would unveil my eyes to see what he wanted me to see. I remember skipping dinner that night and isolating myself from everyone so that I could hear the voice of God. I spent most of the night praying and pleading for God to open my eyes. This continued for several days as I was longing for him to show me my purpose and calling. I believe that prayer and fasting as well as meditation on the word of God is a prerequisite to the answers we seek. I wanted to know his desire and plan for me, and know it without any doubt.

As I spent time in prayer and meditation about this issue, God spoke to me very directly and profoundly. I knew it was his voice. What I needed to do was stop worrying about what I wanted to do and instead ask the Lord what he wanted me to do. I came to understand that is a critical question that we must ask God in order to find out his purpose for our lives. We cannot focus on ourselves but must instead listen to what God wants us to do, for this is the only way to achieve true success and peace. Sometimes it is difficult to listen to what God says to us. For me, the Lord began dealing with me on a very personal and very painful level. He brought all the pain and loneliness and bitterness of my childhood back to me, and I thought not only about my experience but also about the millions of other children in Africa and around the world who go through the same or even worse things than I did. Although I had endured my past and God had blessed me greatly, my heart hurt for the innocent children in the world who die every day never knowing love or happiness or even what it feels like to have a full belly. The despair, the pain—it was so prevalent throughout the world, and why? It seemed senseless that some in the world could have so much while others fought every day just to live.

Even thinking about these things brought the pain of my childhood—losing my parents, fighting for my life—rushing to the surface, but through reliving that pain I realized God had something in store for me. I knew I was going to do something on behalf of the world's poor and hungry. I didn't know how God was going to use me, but my answer to him was, "With your help, I will do what you want me to do, Lord, and go where you want me to go." As time went on, it became clear to me that Isaiah 61:1-3 explains why God brought me to the United States—to equip me for the mission he has called me to do. This passage states:

> *The spirit of the Sovereign Lord is on me, because the Lord has anointed me to preach good news to the poor. He has sent me to bind up the brokenhearted, to proclaim freedom for the captives and release from*

*darkness for the prisoners, to proclaim the year of the
Lord's favor and the day of vengeance of our God, to
comfort all who mourn and provide for those who grieve
in Zion- to bestow on them a crown of beauty instead of
ashes, the oil of gladness instead of mourning, and a
garment of praise instead of a spirit of despair.*

I realized that I was not in America and not in college
for any sort of personal gain. This wasn't about me.
Instead, I was being equipped with the knowledge I
needed to carry out God's plan for me. God had given
me an indescribable passion and desire to fight for the
world's castoffs, and especially for the African people.
Though Jesus reminds us in John 12:8 that, "We will
always have the poor among us," God also instructs us
in Deuteronomy 15:4 that, "There shall be no poor
among us." I knew then that selecting a major would be
easy. I just had to be still and follow what God opened
up to me. I decided to major in economics and minor in
international studies. Understanding economics on both
small and large scales would be essential to my calling,
as would learning about diplomacy—how issues played
out on a global level.

Now that I knew my purpose and calling in life, I
decided to surround myself with professors and
advisors whom I respected for their knowledge and
wisdom. These people were my mentors, not only in my
academic work but also in my personal life. They
challenged me to think critically about issues and they
equipped me to think intellectually. They inspired me to
reach for the sky and not to settle for less or limit
myself. As I spent more time with my mentors and

developed these skills, I realized that this higher level of thinking—looking critically and analytically at issues and questioning the status quo—was part of the reason that Africa lagged so far behind the rest of the world. The people of Africa are generally not encouraged or even allowed to question authority. People are "fed" the answers and never learn how to find things out for themselves. Africa will always be at a disadvantage until we develop the human capital of our citizens, and I believe that education is the foundation.

I also began to seek out more friendships with other students. I had become close with the members of the soccer team, but I wanted to meet as many people as I could. While most students on campus were white, there were also a number of international students. I wanted to find a diverse group of friends, but I noticed that the students tended to hang out most with students of the same background and cultural group. In the cafeteria, the white students would all sit together, the African-American students would all sit together, and the international students were another group. I wondered why everyone couldn't mix together to enjoy a meal. For the first time, I saw myself as "black," and as a minority. It was hard for me to see the segregation that existed between the students. This was new to me because my American family is white and has always loved me and accepted me despite our differences in race and nationality. I couldn't understand why this was such a big issue in the United States. "Why can't we just accept our differences and accept one another for who God created us to be?" I asked myself.

On campus, I didn't feel entirely comfortable with

either the white students or the African-American
students, so I primarily associated with the international
students. Coming in, I thought that the African-
American students and the international African
students would get along because of our mutual
descent. I thought that we were brothers and sisters and
considered the two groups as "one." I guess I was
wrong. They didn't want to have anything to do with
us. We international students were pretty much doing
everything by ourselves—hanging out together, eating
together, and helping each other learn more about the
culture and customs of our new home. As time went on,
I learned about the racial struggle that the United States
had experienced and was continuing to experience. I
thought about this ongoing problem very seriously and
wanted to do something about it before my graduation.
In my mind, the problem was that each racial or ethnic
group was failing to love each other as God loves us and
failing to see each other as God sees us. We formed a
club—at first it was for international students—for
people to come together and talk about the major issues
and daily struggles we were facing as a group.
Eventually, the group got larger and included a diverse
group of students. We discussed sensitive issues such as
race relations on campus, with the intention of helping
students embrace and accept diversity. As the Bible says
in 2 Corinthians 5:18-20: "All this is from God, who
reconciled us to himself through Christ and gave us the
ministry of reconciliation: that God was reconciling the
world to himself in Christ, not counting men's sins
against them. And he has committed to us the message
of reconciliation." Although these efforts didn't totally

eliminate racism on campus, we did see some change as whites, Africans, and African Americans began talking to each other more and sitting together for dinner. Martin Luther King, Jr. was certainly right when he said:

We hate each other because we fear each other, and we fear each other, because we don't know each other and we don't know each other because we are separated from each other, and only by keeping the channels of communication open can we know each other.[6]

In my mind, prejudices are caused or perpetuated by a lack of communication. Throughout world history, the international community has failed to know each other, and therefore has created fear of one another. I believe that many of our world problems could be avoided if we truly knew each other. The solution for international peace and stability is getting to know one another. In the case of our college campus, those students who were open to communication began learning from one another, and their perceptions and attitudes towards one another changed.

In my junior year, I decided to apply to be a hall chaplain. After an interview with the campus pastor, I was accepted into the position, and I was happy to be given that responsibility. As hall chaplain, I devoted a portion of my time to teaching the word of God to students in my hall, mentoring and encouraging others who were going through some tough issues and struggles, and praying with others as we were striving to be the "light and salt" in our hall for others to see. I enjoyed this work, and I wanted to become more active

on campus. Because I felt that one day God was going to
use me to facilitate change in a very big way, I decided
to get involved with change on a small scale. Although
no international student had ever done it and although I
had no idea whether or not people would actually vote
for me, I ran for student senate. I developed a strong
mission statement and launched my campaign.
Surprisingly to me, the student body voted me in. I was
very excited and I made sure to call home and tell Dad
and Mom the news. I was appointed as a committee
member for the cross-cultural studies and honor
committees. Together, along with faculty and staff, we
created guidelines and made important decisions that
affected the entire student population. I was able to
represent my fellow students by bringing their concerns
to the committee members. I used my roles as a hall
chaplain and senator to bridge the gaps between
students, creating a more loving and caring community
and helping students to see one another as children of
God–instead of letting nationalities and race distance us
from God. I maintained these two positions until my
senior year.

The year 2004 was a big one for me. It was my final
year at Bluffton. I was very excited about graduation
and getting a degree, but I knew that I needed to further
my education at the graduate level to better equip
myself for what God has called me to do. I began
searching for a school where I could begin graduate
studies in economic development. Several universities
across the nation offered that course of study, but I was
looking for a university that was Christ-centered and
taught from a Biblical perspective and not just from a

worldview standpoint. This narrowed the search quite a bit. I spent most of my last semester at Bluffton preparing for graduation as well as applying for graduate school. On May 2, 2004, I officially graduated from Bluffton College. I will always remember having my friends and family there to watch me and to celebrate my achievement. I remember my friends screaming my name and the audience applauding as I walked up to get my diploma from the president of Bluffton. Dad and Mom had planned a huge party for me back home. They had to rent a tent to accommodate all the people they invited. I will carry the memory of that day with me forever.

Once all the celebrating was over, I spent the months of May and June waiting and hoping to hear back from the universities where I had applied for graduate school. As time wore on I was nervous that not hearing anything was a bad sign. I tried to think of options if graduate school did not work out, but I knew God would work it out and, by his faithfulness, I heard back from three of the schools that I applied to. After reading more about each school and spending much time in prayer and reflection, I chose to attend Eastern University, even though it was in Pennsylvania, eight hours from Dad and Mom. In July, we visited the campus so that I could see it before making a final commitment to attend. That visit went well, and in August I relocated to St. Davis, Pennsylvania. I was studying for a master of science degree in international economic development, with a concentration in public policy and advocacy. St. Davis was right outside of Philadelphia, so moving there from the tiny town of

Waynesfield was an enormous culture shock. As time went on, I adapted to the environment and culture of the city. Once I was settled, I began tackling my studies, and in the end, my hard work paid off. By the help of God and through hard work and perseverance, I graduated from Eastern on May 31, 2006.

On the night of my graduation, as I was lying on my bed and reflecting over my time at graduate school, the spirit of the Lord came down on me and spoke to me deeply about the grace of God. I started weeping as I thought about his grace in my life. Growing up as a little boy, I never thought or dreamed of going to school at all, but God in his mercy made a way for me to go—even though I was too old to attend school. More than that, upon my arrival in Ouagadougou, he made a way for me to graduate from high school. Despite all the obstacles and oppositions I faced while I was in Africa, out of his mighty hand he brought me to the United States and showed me that nothing is too hard for him. He had shown that he is indeed "Jehovah Jirah," my provider. He has blessed me with grace, far beyond what I could ever think or imagine. As David said it in Psalm 23:5, God has "anointed my head with oil; my cup overflows" with his grace. That night, there were no words to express my thanksgiving and gratitude to him, just complete silence and tears running down my face. I stayed up most of that night, thanking him over and over as I was stirred by the Holy Spirit. I concluded that I was where I was and had what I had not because of my hard work, but because of the grace of God. Through God's grace, I began to see my past experiences as a testimony of God's love and purpose for my life, instead of being ashamed or embarrassed by the things I had to endure. Through that very same grace–a grace that enables me to remove the mask that I had hidden behind for many years–I can look at my past through new eyes.

PART FOUR
MORE THAN AN OVERCOMER

-13-
USING MY PAST FOR THE GLORY OF GOD

They overcame him by the blood of the lamb and by the word of their testimony.
—Revelation 12:11

When I first began visiting the United States with Dad and Mom and traveling around to different churches giving my testimony, I saw that when people heard about the miracles that God had performed in my life, they were encouraged in their faith. God used my story to transform the hearts and minds of many people, and their hearts were filled with compassion for others—especially those less fortunate. At times, people would give me gifts for telling my story, but I was uncomfortable with the idea of "selling" my testimony. It is not that I did not want people's help, but I was more interested in seeing people's hearts become more generous and compassionate to people around the world and not just toward me. I was an ambassador for those who are suffering, and I didn't want people's giving to end with helping only me. I wanted to inspire them to help the voiceless people whom I was representing.

Because of the pain that surfaced in me when I would share my story, and the desire not to "sell" my story, I went through a season of not sharing the full extent of it. Instead of sharing the painful details of my past, I would only give a generalization of what I had gone through in order not to relive completely all the pain. I was embarrassed and ashamed of some of the things I had to do to survive as a little boy, and I didn't want people to know the entire truth. I would just tell people that my life is comparable to the life of Moses or Joseph in the Bible. I felt my life was similar in many ways to those men, and if people could understand Moses and Joseph, they would understand me and would not need to ask me any questions about my life. I avoided answering them when they asked me questions about my past. Instead, I would change the topic to something different. I always had a fear of not knowing how people would react or respond. As a result, many people, even my closest friends, never really knew me and what I had gone through. It was like I was living with a big wall between myself and others. However, God was not okay with this wall that I allowed in my life.

As part of obtaining my master's of science degree, I was required to do an internship in a developing country. After researching many organizations and trying to figure out where to go, I chose to intern with Compassion International—a non-profit organization committed to releasing children from poverty in Jesus' name in Burkina-Faso and around the world. As I was returning from my internship in the Fall of 2005, I felt in my heart that God wanted me to start sharing the full extent of my testimony once again. I realized that sharing my testimony was not about me, but about what God wanted to do through me. Right there at that moment, I asked God to forgive me for my self-centeredness and prayed that he would bless me with enough boldness to share with others the good news of what he has done in my life. From that point on, I made a vow to God to share my story with others—not for my sake, but for the sake of others. I vowed to proclaim the wonders and miracles that God has done in my life so that others will know and believe in him, for he is the one and only true God. I began searching for the best way to share my testimony with people as God has commanded me to do. After some thought, I decided to write a book about my life, as a way to spread the story to people around the world.

In addition to obeying God by sharing my story, I came to discover the tremendous healing that I needed from my past. Without a doubt, writing this book has helped free me from the pain, bitterness, and fear I was holding in my heart. I have learned the power of sharing one's testimony, as an important part of the healing process. This was something I was not willing to do for years, but I am discovering that true healing comes not only through inner forgiveness, but also through sharing the unspeakable past with others. Revelation 12:11 states, "They overcame him by the blood of the lamb and by the word of their testimony." This verse shows that Satan's grip is loosed when we find the strength from God to share our testimony. In other words, both inner forgiveness and outer forgiveness are critical to experiencing the total freedom that God desires us to have.

Without a doubt God has used Dad and Mom to change my world. Unwanted by my friends because of my social and economic conditions, rejected by my own family because of my faith in Jesus Christ, I was embraced into their hearts. From my loneliness they became my closest friends and adopted me as their very own son. While I was craving food to ease my hunger, they fed me—not because they had a lot of wealth but because of their loving, caring and compassionate hearts. The Lord has indeed used them to turn my world upside down.

Many people dream of making the world a better place. Politicians, philosophers, scholars, theologians and many others continue to debate each day about how to change the world, each claiming to have the greatest formula. Though I don't necessarily believe that they are wrong in their thinking, I believe that loving people just the way they are is the most important and powerful weapon we can use to change the world. Believe it or not, the poor, the "forgotten," and the "outcasts" need our friendship and love more than our financial help. From the book of Genesis to Revelation, the Bible is filled with stories about the love of God. The man who molests the young boy or girl has failed to love him or her. The husband who abuses his children and mistreats his wife has failed to love them. The suicide bomber who blows up himself along with hundreds or thousands of innocent men, women and children has failed to love his enemies.

Jesus gave us the greatest commandment in Matthew 22:37-40: "Love the Lord your God with all your heart, and with all your soul and with all your mind. This is the first and greatest commandment. And the second is like it: love your neighbor as yourself. The laws of the prophets hang on these two commandments." I believe your neighbor can be the person next door, or the little girl in the streets searching for a place to lay her head in Palestine, or the woman in Sudan searching for peace, or the boy in Iraq searching for a place to hide from bloodshed in his war-torn country, or the man in Lesotho, South Africa lying on his hard cement floor waiting to die of AIDS, or the rich businessman in the United States. Everybody around the world is our neighbor; we are called to love them all as we love ourselves.

Wherever you are and whatever you have, whether you are educated or not, rich or poor, open your heart to people in need of love. In doing so, you will change the world into a better place to live. Martin Luther King, Jr. said it this way, "Everyone can be great because anyone can serve. You don't have to have a college degree to serve. You don't have to make your subject and your verb agree to serve. You only need a heart full of grace and a soul generated by love."[8]

I believe with all my heart that if we could love each other as we love ourselves, there wouldn't be any genocide, any war, any terrorism, any hunger or starvation in the world, any slavery or apartheid, or any other problem we are dealing with today. If we could love each other as our neighbors, we would literally turn the world upside down—that is the power of love. God opened the eyes of the apostle Paul to capture this vision found in 1 Corinthians 13:

> *If I speak in the tongues of men and of angels, but have not love, I am only a resounding gong or a clanging*

cymbal. *If I have the gift of prophecy and can fathom all mysteries and all knowledge, and if I have a faith that can move mountains, but have not love, I am nothing. If I give all I possess to the poor and surrender my body to the flames, but have not love, I gain nothing....and now these three remain: faith, hope and love. But the greatest is love.*

FINAL REMARKS

Trust in the Lord with all of your heart and lean not on your own understanding, in all of your ways acknowledge him and he will make your paths straight.
                                                                        —Proverbs 3:5-6

Throughout our lives, we will encounter various storms and difficult circumstances. At times, those circumstances seem unbearable, making life seem meaningless. This was exactly how I felt about my own life.

Now that I look back on my life, I have come to the realization that nothing in our lives happens by accident–whether it makes sense or not–and that God is always in control of every event. God is more interested in building our characters than ensuring our comfort. God will take us through the fire to shape and mold us into his own image, while never letting go of our hands. As God forms a new person within us, he is also positioning us step by step to the next level that he wants to take us. The Bible states that "the steps of a righteous man are ordered by God" (Psalm 37:23).

When François was trying to harm me, and ultimately chase me out of the village, it did not make sense to me. It was hard for me to understand why my own family member, who was supposed to be taking care of me, would try to hunt me down like an animal. However, as time went on, I understood that God allowed him to do that in order to position me into the plans he has for my life. After the persecution from François, God led me to an unknown city and brought Francis into my life, who later introduced me to Pastor Paul. Through these people, I was introduced to YFC and later met my mom and dad. Throughout my life, God has consistently brought people to help me at different stages, as he was transitioning me from one level to the next. We can clearly see this in the life of Joseph, as God intentionally allowed many events to happen that appeared to be bad things. God was preparing him for the plans he had for his life.

I have also come to understand that God uses our past and our own personal struggles to reveal his purposes for our lives. God allows us to go through difficult and unthinkable circumstances so that we can later have the passion to help others walk through similar circumstances. Throughout the years, it has become very clear that God allowed me to go through the things that I went through in my childhood not only to shape and mold my character, but also to reveal my purpose in life. I believe that one reason God brought me to the United States was to prepare and equip me to respond to the spiritual, social, and economic needs of the people in Africa and the rest of the world. Through these events and life experiences, he has given me a heart and a passion to reach those who are fatherless, hurting physically or economically, or separated from God.

Without a doubt, we live in a world full of trials and tribulations, grief, sorrow and pain. Let's face it, divorce, unemployment, religious persecution, and death of loved ones, are some of the trials that we experience.

Despite what trials you are going through, hold on to Jesus and trust him with all of your heart. In the end, he will work out everything for your good. Jesus reminds us in John 16:33 that, "In this world you will have trouble. But take heart, I have overcome the world."

As we come to the conclusion of this book, I pray that God will open your heart to love his people regardless of nationality, race, gender and class—as he himself loves them.

This is my prayer for each one of you:

May God bless you with a restless discomfort
about easy answers, half-truths, and superficial
relationships, so that you may seek truth boldly and
love deep within your heart.

May God bless you with holy anger
at injustice, oppression, and exploitation of people,
so that you may tirelessly work for justice, freedom, and
peace among all people.

May God bless you with the tears to shed
with those who suffer from pain, rejection, starvation,
war, or the loss of all that they cherish,
so that you may reach out your hand to comfort them
and transform their pain into joy.

And, may God bless you with enough foolishness
to believe that you really CAN make a difference in this
world, so that you are able, with God's grace, to do
what others claim cannot be done. [9]
Amen!

Endnotes

[1] Clark, Paul L., "It's Difficult Being a Middle Income North American," (non-published letter).

[2] Maria De Jesus, Carolina, *Child of the Dark: The Diary of Carolina Maria de Jesus,* New York: Signet Classic, 2003, p. 37.

[3] Maria de Jesus, *Child of the Dark,* p. 22.

[4] http://www.uneca.org, keyword Burkina-Faso. (accessed on April 15, 2006).

[5] Blackaby, Henry and Blackaby, Richard. *Called to be God's Leader: Lessons from the Life of Joshua.* Nashville, Tennesse: Thomas Nelson, Inc, 2004, p. 2.

[6] Carson, Clayborne, ed., "The papers of Martin Luther King, Jr., Vol. IV: Symbol of the Movement." January 1975-December 1958.

[7] Genesis 22:14.

[8] http://www.studentlife.uoguelph.ca/citizencommunity/documents/communityinvolmentquotations.pdf Quotations on Community Involvement, Service, and Volunteerism. Martin Luther King Jr., Civil Rights Leader, (accessed on February 24, 2007).

[9] Yancey, Philip, *Prayer: Does It Make Any Difference?* Grand Rapids, Michigan: Zondervan, 2006, p. 105.

About the Author

 Jean-Paul is an ordained minister and serves the body of Christ in various capacities through preaching, teaching, as a life coach, and as a one-on-one discipleship coach. He has experience working within diverse congregational, corporate, educational and community contexts. Jean-Paul also serves as the President & Chief Executive Officer of Kingdom Investment International, a non-profit organization committed to promoting sustainable economic development in Africa. He holds a bachelor's degree in Economics and International Studies from Bluffton University (Bluffton, Ohio) and a Master of Science in International Economic Development with an emphasis in Public Policy from Eastern University (Eastern University). He has appeared on several radio and television programs sharing his life story and advocating on behalf of others in less developed nations. Jean-Paul has been married to Rita for 12 years, and the Lord has blessed them with two beautiful children, Moriah (7) and Caleb (5). The Tiendrebeogo family resides in Bellefontaine, Ohio.

Jean-Paul is available for speaking engagements.
He can be reached at:
www.kingdominvestment.org

WA